W9-CZM-357

J. M. HODGES LEARNING CENTER
WHARTON COUNTY JUNIOR COLLEGE
WHARTON, TEXAS 77488

Texas:

Amazing
But True

Jack Maguire

067310

EAKIN PRESS
Austin, Texas

U. M. HODGES LEARNING CENTER
WHARTON COUNTY JUNIOR COLLEGE
WHARTON, TEXAS 77488

Library of Congress Cataloging in Publication Data

Maguire, Jack, 1919—
    Texas: amazing but true.

    Includes index.
    1. Texas—History, Local—Addresses, essays, lectures.
I. Title.
F386.5.M33   1984   976.4   84–18647
ISBN 0-89015-497-2

FIRST EDITION

Copyright © 1984
By Jack Maguire

Published in the United States of America
By Eakin Press, P.O. Box 23066, Austin, Texas 78735

ALL RIGHTS RESERVED

84-18647

976.4
M276T

0C7310

DEDICATION

To my wife Pat,

who insisted that I write it;

And to my sons, Jack and Kevin,

and their wives, Margaret and Gay,

with the hope that they will enjoy reading it;

And to Christopher, my grandson,

who may appreciate it one day.

iii

Table of Contents

Acknowledgments

Writing a book is a project that always involves a great many people besides the author and many had a role in making *Texas: Amazing, but True* a reality.

My special thanks goes to Al Mogavero, publisher of *Southwest Airlines Magazine*, and his associate and editor, Kenneth E. Lively, who published most of the articles in their original form in that outstanding publication.

Some of the photographs were supplied by my life-long friend and first editor, Claud Easterly, of The Denison (Texas) *Herald*, from his personal files. Tom Shelton, curator of the outstanding historical photo collection at The University of Texas Institute of Texan Cultures in San Antonio, was of invaluable help in locating many of the illustrations.

To Pat Maguire, my wife and writing partner for so many years, I owe a special debt. She not only helped me research many of these stories, but served as my editor who put the material in form for this book. And we both owe thanks to our friend and neighbor, Fred Stefan of Fredericksburg, who made our task easier by graciously offering his personal copier to us on many weekends at our home in that historic town.

In a sense, this book is theirs as well as mine because it would not have been possible without them.

Preface

Through no fault of our own, we Texans are functional illiterates when it comes to the history of this remarkable state.

How many of us ever learned from our textbooks that a Texan built and flew the first airplane thirty-eight years before the Wright brothers? Or that the capitol and government of Missouri once were located in East Texas? Or that Santa Anna should be remembered not just for his dirty work at the Alamo? He also had a role in giving chewing gum to the world.

Few of us were taught that Texas is the only state that may not own its capitol. Or that the Civil War ended here, not in Virginia. Or that Texas celebrated the first Thanksgiving long before the Pilgrims even arrived.

These true stories, and others like them, make up this book. They have been gathered during more than forty years of research during which I have tried to find the odd, unusual, bizarre and humorous — but true — stories about Texas as it was, and is.

For a decade, the results of this research have appeared each month as articles in *Southwest Airlines Magazine.* Of the more than one hundred such stories published thus far, these included in this book are among those the readers of the magazine liked best. My hope is that you also will enjoy them, and that they will tell you some things about Texas that you never knew until now.

Jack Maguire

San Antonio, Texas
June, 1984

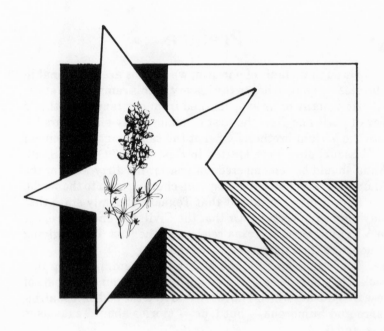

The Wonderful World That's Texas

Texans are just now beginning to discover how right the late George Sessions Perry was when he described their state "as a world in itself."

Where else, except Texas, can one visit a park that is only twelve feet wide and twenty-one feet long? Or walk through a forest of oak trees that never grow higher than thirty inches? Or ride a railroad whose entire 22.5 miles of right-of-way is a park? Or stop by a "zoo" that has almost 300 species of the same animal?

Discovering the unique things about Texas has been a pastime since 1514. That year, Alonzo Alvarez de Pineda, inspired by reports of the discovery of America by Columbus only twenty-seven years before, stopped off on the Texas coast and insured a place in history as the first tourist. Unfortunately the Spanish explorer found little activity to excite him so he spent his time mapping the area. However, he started a trend that continues to bring visitors to Texas in ever increasing numbers.

Although the sights of Texas have been on the agenda of some tourists for more than 400 years, the state showed little interest in them until about sixty years go. Tourism as a business really got its start in 1921 when the voters elected as their governor a man who loved nature. He was Pat M. Neff, a Waco lawyer, and one plank in his platform called for giving Texas a

The graves of Davy Crockett's widow, and son Robert, comprise all there is of Acton State Park, the smallest state park in the world.

—Archives Division, Texas State Library

system of state parks. The idea didn't excite the people very much, but in 1923, he did convince the Legislature to create a state parks board. However, they refused to appropriate any salary for the members and gave them no funds with which to buy potential parkland.

Governor Neff was not a man to give up on a dream. He hauled his touring car out of the Executive Mansion garage and drove 8,000 miles around the state making one hundred and ten speeches in behalf of parks. When he returned to Austin, he had talked Texans into donating fifty-two different tracts worth more than $1 million and all dedicated as parks. Today Texas has one hundred and three state parks and recreation areas and more than fifteen hundred roadside parks along its highways. It also has two national parks, plus numerous historic sites and memorials. There are ten national wildlife refuges in Texas. They offer everything from a 67.5 mile continuous beach on Padre Island to a moored U.S. Navy battleship and a quarry where Indians made weapons 10,000 years ago.

It is the uniqueness of Texas parks, not necessarily their numbers and superior facilities, that will attract upwards of sixteen million visitors in a given year. Take the Odessa Meteor Crater, for example.

There are only two places in the U.S. where meteor craters exist. To see one, the visitor must travel either to Arizona or to a spot in Texas eight miles south and west of Odessa. More than 20,000 years ago, a cluster of these "falling stars" struck this site in the now oil-rich Permian Basin. The impact was so great that 4.3 million cubic feet of rock was expelled or shifted, forming a crater 500 feet wide and nearly 100 feet deep. Today the crater is a scientific and historical attraction that is rare in the world.

Strangely enough, it isn't a state park at all. It is operated by the local meteorological society.

For the Texas explorer whose interests run to animals instead of meteorology, the zoo at Victoria is a must. There the crowd pleasers in what may be the world's most unusual zoo aren't lions, tigers or monkeys. They're native Texans.

Victoria's zoo is as Texan as cowboys and oil derricks because the more than 170 animals represent more than 80 species that are native to the state. Included are endangered spe-

3

cies that Texans rarely see in the wild, like the prairie chicken, the ocelot, the fox and the alligator. The ten-acre zoo is designed to provide the animals an environment like their natural habitat and there are few cages. It is one of the few places where one can pet a razorback hog, usually one of the most vicious animals encountered by hunters. This one is so people-oriented that he delights in having his ears pulled.

For unusual zoos, however, the one at The University of Texas at Austin wins hands down. It claims to be the world's largest zoo devoted to one animal because all of its residents are fruit flies. Almost 300 species of what scientists know as the genera *Drosophila* are maintained in more than 3,000 vials. The tiny flies may hold little interest for the casual visitor, but they are of great importance in research. The University has been collecting them for more than fifty years and now has about ninety-five percent of all known species in the world.

For the rock hound, there is a roadside park on Highway 166 in Jeff Davis County that has special interest. It is called Rockpile Park and it is just that — a pile of pink rock slabs that reach as high as a three-story building and cover more than an acre. Many of the stones have been highly polished. Legend says they got that way from generations of Indian women using them for stretching and drying deer and buffalo hides.

Rockpile Park is not far from another sight to delight the traveler — the McDonald Observatory of The University of Texas. One of the largest observatories in the country, and the only one in Texas, the welcome mat is always out for visitors. At the Visitors' Center, there are many exhibits of the wild, blue yonder. On certain evenings of the week, visitors are even invited in to view the heavens through the observatory telescopes.

Perhaps not as old as the galaxies one can see at McDonald, but equally as interesting, is the spot where dinosaurs once roamed. Located just outside of Glen Rose, and within easy driving distance of Fort Worth, is the bed of the Paluxy River with dozens of tracks left by beasts that occupied that area 100 million years ago. It was not until 1880 that they were discovered by a rancher in the area and it was not until 1930 that several of the tracks were removed for display in museums. The area became a state park in 1969 and has become a visitor's mecca since.

4

Dinosaurs may have been resident around Glen Rose, but in the area to the west, the prairie dog once outnumbered everything else. As late as 1903, it was estimated that a billion of the tiny animals that appear to be related both to the squirrel and the rat lived in colonies in Texas. Today an estimated 1.5 million people annually journey to Lubbock, one of the state's fastest growing cities, to visit one of the largest prairie dog towns still extant.

At one time, Lubbock was the center of a prairie dog colony that spread over 37,000 square miles and counted some 400 million residents. In later years, ranchers and farmers almost exterminated the pesky animal (they vary from twelve to fifteen inches in length and weigh two to three pounds) and they were fast disappearing when Mr. and Mrs. K.N. Clapp set aside a seven-acre reservation for them several years ago. Today they are Lubbock's outstanding tourist attraction.

From a prairie dog down to the world's largest land-locked ocean is only a half day's drive or a quick flight in Texas. Arlington, between Dallas and Fort Worth, is a long way from the coast, but it boasts dolphins, whales and other creatures of the sea in a thirty-five acre park it built to house them. It required 2.5 million gallons of water to create a world of exotic birds, of pirate ships and sea lions, but they're all just off the old turnpike in Arlington.

Actually Arlington's oceanarium contains all of the seven seas. Miniatures of the Mediterranean, the Indian Ocean and the Sea of Cortez, plus the other four, were all created by a "brine maker" that uses powdered salt and chemicals to manufacture sea water. Now it's the only place in Texas where the visitor can sail around the world without ever leaving the state.

There are no lighthouses at Arlington's Seven Seas, but they still exist along the Texas coast. One of the best preserved is the Port Isabel light across the ship channel from the eastern tip of Galveston Island. The lighthouse was built in 1872 and used through 1934. It is easily reached by a short ferry ride.

From lighthouses to land-locked oceans to prairie dog towns, there are 1,001 sights in the wonderful world of Texas. There is a wilderness only one hundred and thirty miles from Houston and sixty miles from San Antonio known as Palmetto State Park which may be one of the most beautiful natural areas in the nation. There is the Sauer-Beckmann homestead, now a part of the Lyndon B. Johnson State Park near Fredericksburg, where every day is lived as it was in the early 1900s. And in the fall, deep in the Hill Country of Bandera County, still another state park (one of the newest) shows off the Lost Maples of the Sabinal — a stand of these beautiful trees that somehow belong in New England, not Texas.

And what about that park that is only twelve feet wide and twenty-one feet long? It's called Acton and it's in a village cemetery at the intersection of Highways 208 and 190 in Hood County. It's the burial place of the widow of David Crockett, hero of the Alamo, and of his son, Robert, a soldier in the army of the Republic of Texas. It is said to be the smallest state park in the world.

The Texas State Railroad is the only railway in the world that is, itself, a park. It runs from Rusk to Palestine in East Texas and it operates a daily train powered by a steam engine through some of the most beautiful forests in the state.

Forests, however, aren't limited to East Texas. At Monahans, famous for sand dunes that look for all the world like the Sahara Desert, there is a 40,000-acre forest that many visitors never see. It is one of the largest oak forests in the nation, but all of the trees are Harvard Oaks and they rarely grow more than thirty-six inches high. They are so tiny that viewers of the sand dunes often overlook them.

Of all the sights to be seen in the wonderful world of Texas, however, the San Jacinto Battleground State Historical Park may have the most unique. Here, in a special slip in the shadow of the San Jacinto Monument (highest in the state), rests the U.S. Navy Battleship, *Texas*. A veteran of both World Wars I and II, the *Texas* has been permanently moored at San Jacinto since 1948. She is the last of the dreadnought class of battleships and in her engine room is the last existing ship/piston engine in the world.

This is a glimpse of only a few of the wonders of Texas which that first tourist, Alonzo Alvarez de Pineda, never saw when he stopped off here almost five centuries ago. It's too bad that he can't return now and see what has happened to Texas since.

Who Really Owns
The Texas Capitol?

For almost a century, Texas government has been head-quartered in a Capitol it may not own, located on land to which the state has never had a clear title. And the building itself, although officially opened on May 17, 1888, still isn't completed!

Legally the state probably owns the big, red granite Capitol at the head of Congress Avenue in Austin. It traded three million acres of west Texas lands to a Chicago syndicate in full payment for the construction, although it didn't get a deed to the building until thirty-seven years later. Up to now, the governments of the Republic of Texas and the state have paid three separate claimants for the land on which the Capitol is located. Nevertheless, clear title to the property is not held by the state and never has been.

The question of who really owns the Capitol of Texas goes back to the days when Mexico ruled Texas and one of that government's judges named Thomas Jefferson Chambers. At that time, Mexico had the quaint custom of allowing its justices to take their pay either in cash or real estate and Chambers was a promoter at heart. He knew that land values could only go up as more settlers arrived in Texas, so he elected to take his fees in acreage instead of money.

Chambers, a colorful and controversial Texan who later was to become a general in the revolution against Mexico and who would make four unsuccessful tries for the governorship

Thomas Jefferson Chambers was the first to claim title to the land on which the Capitol in Austin is located. In 1925, his daughters sold their rights to the property to the State of Texas for $20,000, but the title still isn't clear.

—Photo courtesy The Institute of Texan Cultures

Texas built its first Capitol in Austin on land to which the state did not have clear title. When this building burned, the present Capitol was built on the same site. After more than a century, there is still a question as to who really owns the land.

after Texas became a state, thought big. With the approval of the Mexican government, he got as much free land as he could. His huge tract started on the north bank of the Colorado River on the western outskirts of the present city of Austin, then extended thirteen miles northeast to a point just below Round Rock in Williamson County. The tract's western boundary ran south back to the river through the eastern edge of today's Austin. The tract included the land where the Texas Capitol now stands.

Because these Mexican land grants were also guaranteed by the constitution of the new Republic of Texas, Chambers was in no hurry to record the title to his property. At the time all of the tract was located in Bastrop County (Travis and Williamson Counties were not carved out until later) and he should have recorded the title in the Bastrop Land Office. His failure to do so is the basis for Texas's troubles today over who owns its Capitol.

After the 1836 revolution, in which Chambers was commissioned a major general in the Texan Army, land-hungry settlers began to pour in just as he had predicted. The Bastrop County Land Office, having no record of his claim to any lands, began granting new settlers large chunks out of the Chambers tract. About the same time, the Republic of Texas started looking for a site for its permanent capitol.

On January 14, 1839, the Congress of the Republic passed, and President Mirabeau B. Lamar approved, "An Act for the permanent Location of the Seat of Government." The Act provided for five commissioners selected by Congress to find a site "between the rivers Trinidad (Trinity) and Colorado, and above the Old San Antonio Road." If the site chosen was not public property and a sale could not be negotiated, the Act empowered the Republic to condemn the land and pay the owners a reasonable price.

By March 23, the commissioners had selected as their choice an area that now comprises much of the central city of Austin and was a part of the original grant to Chambers. However more than a year earlier, the Bastrop County Land Office had patented about 1,500 acres of the same real estate chosen for the capitol city to one Samuel Gocher or Goucher, a farmer living a few miles downriver. The Goucher portion included the hill on which the present Capitol was to be built almost a half century later.

Within a few months after Goucher had received his patent, however, the entire family was slaughtered by Indians. At least, that was the thought at the time. So with the Gouchers supposedly dead and no obvious heirs around to claim their lands, a couple of real estate promoters named Edward Burleson and Joseph Porter Brown filed a claim for it. The Land Office gave its approval and Burleson and Brown promptly sold it to the Republic of Texas. By the end of the year, the Republic had purchased or condemned the land it wanted and the city of Austin was chartered December 27, 1839.

Meanwhile, General Chambers, who had been living at his place at Round Point, Liberty County, and not paying too much attention to the efforts to find a site for the capitol, in 1840 finally got around to filing his claim. When he discovered that

10

the Bastrop county Land Office had already handed out 150 separate patents on land that was wholly or partly within his original tract, General Chambers went on the attack. He began filling lawsuits against any and everybody who claimed any part of what he believed to be rightfully his. However, the Republic of Texas, falling back on its constitutional right not to be sued without the express permission of the government, ignored Chambers and went ahead with its plans to erect the first Capitol.

The general had no idea, however, of either surrendering or retreating and he kept his lawsuits alive. Although the Legislature, after Texas became a state in 1845, continued to refuse him permission to sue, the Supreme court in 1858 did rule that Chambers had as perfect a title to his lands "as the law is capable of bestowing." He continued his legal fight until March 15, 1865, when he was killed by an assassin's bullet as he sat in the library of his home, "Chambersea," at Anahuac, in the Gulf coast county named for him.

The night Chambers was murdered, he was holding his six-month-old daughter, Stella, on his knee. Stella and her older sister, Katie, were to grow up and continue to battle for the titles to the Chambers lands for another sixty years. But before they were old enough to carry on the fight the Goucher claim on the capitol site was resurrected.

It developed that not all of the Gouchers had been murdered by the Indians after all. Three of the Goucher children had been kidnapped, later ransomed and had grown up unaware that their father had patented a tract of land not far from their old home. A daughter, Jane, married, bore some children and died about 1850. A son, James, died in 1849 without ever taking a bride. Another son, William, was alive in 1853 when one E.M. Smith discovered the Goucher claim and saw in it the possibility of turning a fast buck.

He approached William Goucher, the only survivor by then, and offered him $500 for a quit claim deed to the tract. In those days, $500 was a lot of money for a mere 1,500 acres and William was both poor and illiterate. He took the cash and signed the deed with his mark. Smith, with a valid deed in hand, got the Legislature in 1857 to grant him permission to sue the state for the condemnation award allowed under the law. Before the case could get into court, however, the Civil

War intervened and Smith's claim wasn't adjudicated until April 1, 1867. Finally, on June 22, 1872, the court ruled that Smith did, indeed, have a valid claim to the land on which the Capitol was located. In 1874, the Legislature authorized payment of the judgment.

Settlement of Smith's claim left Texas's title to its capitol far from clear. Once the Chambers daughters were grown and married, both continued to press their family's case. They were Mrs. Stella MacGregor and Mrs. Kate Sturgis of Galveston and one of their friends and staunch supporters was none other than Governor James Stephen Hogg.

Hogg was convinced that the sisters actually owned the Capitol grounds but failed in his efforts to get the Legislature to permit them to sue the state. This was true despite the fact that, in 1884 when construction of the present Capitol was started, the sisters had filed a legal notice claiming that since they owned the grounds, they also would own any improvements built on them.

After Hogg left the governor's office, he continued his interest in the case. At one point, he suggested that the sisters build a log cabin on the Capitol grounds and move into it. He assured them that he would defend them in any legal actions brought by the state to oust them. However, Mrs. MacGregor and Mrs. Sturgis vetoed the idea as being beneath their dignity as gentlewomen.

Two decades later, still trying to get title to their lands, the sisters were introduced to R.E. Cofer, an Austin attorney. Once he examined their file of petitions, he was convinced that they had a case. Writing about it later in the October, 1931, issue of the *Texas Law Review*, Cofer said:

"I had not read 30 minutes until I saw these women just as certainly owned the Capitol and its grounds as I owned my own home."

When the 39th Legislature convened in 1925, Cofer was ready to present the case of the two sisters again. This time the arguments presented by Cofer and the attorneys assisting him were persuasive. John Davis, the senator from Dallas, was won over early. In the debate, he warned his colleagues that "Chambers' daughters could come marching up Capitol Hill with the sheriff in front, armed with a writ of possession, to take over the Capitol." He went on to say: "In my judgment as a lawyer the state has a chance to settle a dangerous claim for a small sum."

And a small sum it was, considering the value today of the twenty-five acres on which the Capitol sits. For only $20,000, the sisters agreed to deed the Capitol and its grounds to the state.

Thus for the third time in a century, Texas had paid again for the land and the Capitol it built on it. Yet the title to the property is still under a cloud. Experts in land law point out that while the claim of the Chambers family has been settled, that of the Goucher family has not. Samuel Goucher had three children, yet one son and one daughter did not sign a quit claim deed to their share of his property.

Under the law the descendants of James and Jane Goucher might still have a valid claim to the Capitol of Texas — or at least to the land on which it stands. So it is possible that somewhere in Texas today there are descendants of the Goucher son or daughter who own the Capitol and don't know it.

If they come forward and prove their claim, however, they might end up acquiring a building that is unfinished. The original plans for the Capitol, which is second only to the National Capitol in Washington in size, called for it to be larger than it is. Each of the side entrances was designed to have two-storied, columned porticoes.

Why they were never added is one of history's mysteries.

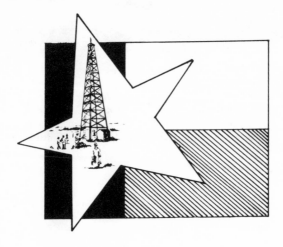

The Reverend Burrell Cannon got his idea for building an airplane after reading the Book of Ezekiel, so he named his company after the prophet who inspired it.

—From an exhibit in the Institute of Texan Cultures, San Antonio

14

The Airship
Inspired by the *Bible*

Late one evening when this century was new, the Reverend Burrell Cannon sat in his study adjoining the Baptist Church in Pittsburg, Camp County, Texas, poring over the Book of Ezekiel.

"Now it came to pass," said the text in Brother Cannon's *Bible*, "as I was among the captives by the River Chebar, the heavens were opened and I saw visions. Out of the fire came four creatures, and the living creatures ran and returned as the appearance of a flash of lightning. And their work was as it were a wheel in the middle of a wheel."

To Preacher Cannon, who held a degree in mechanics from Mississippi College and whose ministry had always been a sideline to his love of inventing gadgets, the Prophet Ezekiel seemed to be speaking directly to him. It was as if the Holy Scriptures were revealing to him and him alone the key that would permit man to fly like a bird.

Brother Cannon read on:

"The appearance of the wheels and their work was like unto the color of a beryl; and the four had one likeness. When they went they went upon their four sides; and they turned not when they went.

"And when the living creatures went, the wheels went by them; and when the living creatures were lifted up from the earth, the wheels were lifted up.

15

"And under the firmament were their wings straight, the one toward the other; every one had two, which covered on that side, their bodies. And when they went, I heard the noise of their wings, like great waters."

Before Brother Cannon laid his *Bible* aside and retired, he had read through the entire book of Ezekiel. And the next day he set about forming the Ezekiel Airship Company with one goal in mind: To use the words of the Prophet and build a winged vehicle in which man might soar verily into the Heavens.

Burrell Cannon was well past middle age when he started his venture, but his unswerving confidence in *Bible* prophecy made him certain of success. He was only a small town preacher but he had a large flock and the confidence of the community. Most important of all, he knew that God was on his side.

Modern aerospace engineers would scoff at anyone naive enough to try to build an airship from the sketchy plans written down by a seer who believed that only angels could fly. Indeed scientists today, after giving the Book of Ezekiel a close reading, believe that it may be an account of the sighting of a UFO —an unidentified flying object that may, incredibly, have been a space vehicle or, more likely, a strange phenomenon produced by atmospheric conditions.

Brother Cannon, however, had no doubts. Within a matter of days, he had convinced P.W. Thorsell, owner of the Pittsburg Foundry, to give him mechanics and space in which to build the airship. A little later in 1901, he chartered the Ezekiel Airship Manufacturing Company, sold Thorsell $13,000 worth of stock at $25 a share and peddled another $7,000 in shares to other Pittsburg citizens.

On May 31, 1901, the Reverend Cannon was far enough along with his plans that he filed for two patents for his machine. One was for what he called a "wind wheel" —a device not unlike the present autogiro. Actually they were "wheels within wheels" as described by Ezekiel and were equipped with vanes to give them lifting power. They were geared to the engine. Theoretically the wheels were to lift the machine off the ground and the vanes, or wings, were to serve as gliders.

The second patent was for a marine propeller, but it had little relationship to the modern aircraft prop. Burrell's propeller was designed as a steering mechanism and not to provide forward thrust for the machine by pulling in air. As it later developed, this may have been his most serious engineering mistake. The lack of a propeller meant that his airship was never able to negotiate altitude nor remain long in flight.

Once the plans were complete, construction of the machine began. Thorsell assigned his top mechanic, Burrell Stamps, to the project. The fact that he and the minister shared the same first name was a curious coincidence; they were not related. The Reverend Cannon and another mechanic, Rowe Lockett, assisted Stamps and apparently there were strong disagreements as the airship was being put together. Stamps, who actually did most of the work, wanted a cast iron engine and propellers like those on today's aircraft. Preacher Cannon vetoed both ideas, however, and insisted on having final approval on each bit of construction.

By the spring of 1902, the aircraft was finished. Several Pittsburg residents of that time, interviewed many years ago, insist that Orville and Wilbur Wright who were destined to become the first recognized aviators, came to see Cannon's plane under construction. Some insist that the Wrights offered Cannon a partnership in their own enterprise. However, neither the few existing contemporary accounts nor material on the Wrights at the Smithsonian Institution in Washington make any mention of their interest in the minister's project. It appears likely that they never saw his airship or ever met the inventor. In fact no one with any knowledge of aerodynamics was on hand when the Reverend Cannon decided to take his plane off the ground.

Even the exact date of the attempt has been lost to history. The attempted flight probably took place late in the spring of 1902, but eyewitnesses (of which several were interviewed in the 1960s) disagreed as to the month. What is known is the fact that it was necessary to tear out a wall of the foundry and use a block and tackle to lower the plane from the second-floor room where it had been built. All witnesses agree on that point.

The airship had a wingspan of from fifteen to twenty feet and was shorter than it was wide. The framework was metal and the rest of the vehicle was wood, probably ash or hickory. The wings were covered with canvas and heavily coated with shellac. They resembled a folding fan because they were folded to the side of the airship when not in use and locked in an unfolded position when the vehicle was in flight.

The craft had four sets of wheels — two in front and two in back. There were two outer wheels about six feet high and between them was a fan with paddles which sucked and pushed the air in the desired direction. The pilot controlled the pitch of the paddles and thus could move the plane forward, backward and up and down. The Reverend Cannon's plans have been lost, but it appears that the airship was powered by a two-cylinder gasoline engine developing 80 horsepower.

The pilot sat in the middle of the craft with the control levers either next to him or directly in front — those who remember seeing the plane aren't sure. They do agree, however, that the man who attempted to fly it that day on a meadow outside of Pittsburg was Stamps, the mechanic who built it.

There is no doubt that the airship got off the ground. According to Stamps, he revved up the engine while several men pushed it about ten feet. At that point, the craft became airborne and flew an estimated ten feet above the ground. Stamps's version was that the plane began to vibrate so violently that he became nervous and brought it back to earth after flying some sixty feet. Other witnesses say that the plane got off the ground but flew less than half that distance. Estimates were that the speed attained was between forty and fifty miles per hour.

At any rate, the first attempt at flight was rated a rousing success by the Reverend Cannon, Stamps and the stockholders of the Ezekiel Airship Manufacturing Company. By the time of the flight, at least one foreign government — that of Germany — had expressed interest in the project. It was rumored that the Germans offered $100,000 for the airship and the right to manufacture it, but there is no record that such an offer was ever made.

Cannon did, however, receive offers of additional backing from a manufacturer in St. Louis. In the spring of 1903, he loaded his airship on a railroad flatcar and his family on a passenger train and headed north. At Texarkana, however, a hurricane struck the freight train and the airship was blown off the car and demolished.

With his craft destroyed, the Reverend Cannon needed money. He went to work as a foreman in a Texarkana sawmill and started building up his savings. Meanwhile Orville and Wilbur Wright had made themselves a place in history with their flight at Kitty Hawk, North Carolina, on December 17, 1903, but Cannon was still convinced his *Ezekiel* was a superior aircraft. In 1908 or 1909, he moved to Longview and started another airship company.

About 1910 he was invited to Chicago where he built another airship. This plane also flew successfully. After it landed, however, the pilot ran into a light pole and knocked off a wing. Disgusted, the Reverend Cannon returned to Longview, quit making airplanes and started working on trying to invent an automatic cotton picker. He formed a $60,000 stock company to promote that invention, but when he died August 9, 1923, in Marshall, the invention was only half finished. He is buried in Grace Hill Cemetery in Longview in an unmarked grave.

Today, except for some musty records in the U.S. Patent Office, there is little to remind the world of the Baptist preacher who might have been remembered as the father of aviation. The foundry where he built his airship still stands in Pittsburg, but the records of the Ezekiel Airship Manufacturing company have disappeared along with the dreams of the man who founded it.

In a sense, however, the airship inspired by the *Bible* is fulfilled prophecy today. The helicopter is a direct descendant of what the Prophet Ezekiel had in mind all along.

This plaque in the Palo Duro Canyon of the Panhandle proclaims to all of the world where the First Thanksgiving observance really took place.

—Photo by Jack Maguire

How Texas Beat the Pilgrims
To the First Thanksgiving

Forget the legend that the Pilgrims gave America its traditional Thanksgiving holiday. The history books are all wrong about that.

Of course there was a day of Thanksgiving celebrated by those early settlers on the Massachusetts coast. The Pilgrims, grateful for the bounty of God that had brought them safely to Plymouth Rock in 1620, certainly did prepare a feast of celebration and gratitude. But seventy-nine years before the Pilgrims ever set out for the New World, the First Thanksgiving already had been celebrated in what is now a Texas park.

In fact, Thanksgiving has had an unusual history in Texas. Perhaps it's because Texans are notorious noncomformists, even in the matter of holidays. Sam Houston, although he never took organized religion very seriously, always felt that the greatest blessing Texas ever received was its independence from Mexico in 1836. So in 1842, when somebody suggested to old Sam that the Republic of Texas should observe one day of Thanksgiving each year, he agreed.

If Texans were going to be thankful, however, Houston wanted them to do it on March 2 — Texas Independence Day. When he proclaimed the holiday in 1842, he announced that it would be a dual celebration of freedom and thanksgiving.

Another eight years passed before there was another Thanksgiving Day in Texas. After almost a decade as an inde-

21

pendent Republic, Texas had joined the Union in 1845. Five years later, Governor Peter H. Bell decided that the state should have an annual day of Thanksgiving. Like Houston, however, he wanted it on, or near, Texas Independence Day. Since March 2 was often celebrated with much drink and the shooting of pistols and even cannon, the Governor wisely moved Thanksgiving Day one week forward. Thus March 7 became the official Thanksgiving Day in 1850.

This, however, came 309 years after that first Thanksgiving ceremony was held in what is now Texas — and 330 years after the Pilgrims were erroneously credited by historians with originating this national holiday.

That first Thanksgiving celebrated on the North American continent happened on May 9, 1541. The site was the Palo Duro Canyon, a giant hole gouged in the red soil of the Panhandle more than 250 million years ago. Francisco Vasquez de Coronado had led his men up from Mexico in search of a legendary city called Quivera — a place so grand and so rich that women were said to cook their food in pots of pure gold.

Instead of one of the seven golden cities which legend said were north of the Rio Grande, Coronado found only limitless plains — flat, grassy lands that seemed to be never-ending. Then, after days of monotonous travel when water was hard to find and provisions ran low, the expedition stumbled onto a gorge more than 1,000 feet deep in places and with a flowing river at the bottom. They also found a tribe of Tejas Indians living on the canyon floor — Indians who were friendly and gave them food.

To celebrate his good fortune, Coronado ordered a day of Thanksgiving. He probably didn't call it that, though. Being a good Catholic, the rite he actually held probably was the Feast of the Ascension conducted by the faithful forty days after Easter. But it was a service of Thanksgiving, conducted by Fray Juan de Padilla. And although the actual date of the celebration wasn't recorded by Coronado, it probably was on May 29 — the day he and his men found the oasis that Palo Duro Canyon proved to be.

To the Texas Society of the Daughters of the American Colonists, at least, Coronado's feast was the first Thanksgiving ever held on this continent. In 1959, the Daughters erected a plaque in the 15,000 acre canyon to proclaim to the world that it was here in the Panhandle of Texas, not at Plymouth Rock in Massachusetts, that the first Thanksgiving Day was observed.

Several years ago, the monument erected by the Daughters was destroyed by vandals. In 1973, the Texas Historical Survey Commission replaced it with an official historical marker. The new marker calls the story merely a "legend" but most Texans prefer to take Coronado's word that it really happened.

After all, he was there.

Keene: The Town
Where Crime is Unknown

Keene, Texas, wasn't settled until 336 years after Sir Thomas More wrote his novel describing an imaginary island where everything and everybody was perfect. Yet Keene, whose 3,013 residents are the first to admit that they and their community haven't achieved perfection, nevertheless comes close to being the kind of place that More imagined his *Utopia* to be.

There are few, if any, towns like Keene in the world. It has no jail, no police, no courts, no divorces and no record of crime since it was settled in 1852. There has never been a strike, a fight, a boisterous crowd, an unseemly scuffle or a profane word uttered, in the memory of any of Keene's citizens.

Like many another Texas community, Keene is a college town but no yells arise from the stadium. There is no stadium because competitive sports like football and baseball aren't allowed. Neither is there a favorite hangout where the college crowd goes to drink beer. None of the 700 students at Southwestern Union College drinks anything stronger than water. Even coffee and tea are taboo.

Keene is full of surprises for the casual visitor. Stop there on a Sunday morning (it's tucked in a fold of the North Texas prairie about forty miles southwest of Dallas) and you'll find the modern, 1400-seat church silent and empty. But drop into the post office and you'll find it open — the only post office in Texas, by the way, that is in full operation on Sundays.

The supermarkets are open on Sundays, too, but they won't hold much interest for the visiting shopper. One reason is that they don't sell meat. Nine out of ten residents of Keene have never tasted meat. Even the hot dogs sold at the diner on Old Betsy Road are made of textured protein, a soybean derivative that can be flavored to taste like beef, chicken, ham or turkey. Also the town's pizza parlor uses textured protein in its spicy offerings.

Neither do Keene's vegeterians believe the old saw that holds that "diamonds are a girl's best friend." All kinds of jewelry (except plain wrist watches) are taboo and there is only one place in town where one can buy a package of cigarettes or a parcel of pipe tobacco.

If Keene sounds like something out of *Brigadoon*, don't believe it. It's a busy, industrious town — but it takes its religion more seriously than most. Its first settlers were Methodists, but in 1890, the Seventh Day Adventist Church located its Southwestern Union College there. Today ninety-five percent of the population are Adventists who observe their church's strong taboos against alcohol, tobacco, dancing and the eating of meat.

When Keene became the center of the Adventist faith in Texas, there was no intention to establish a Utopia. The only purpose was to build a college on a farm in the rolling hills eight miles from Cleburne, in Johnson County. But a town insisted on springing up around the little campus and the citizens were tolerated so long as they kept the tenets of the faith. Even the town's charter grants it special dispensation to work full blast on Sundays and to observe Saturday, the old Hebrew Sabbath, as a day of rest.

Despite its constant growth and the influx of some light industry, Keene's observance of the Adventist ban against practices that the church regards as sinful is still almost total. Playing cards is still outlawed, along with dominoes and other possible games of chance.

There is a beauty shop where women may have their hair shampooed, cut or waved. Lipstick and other makeup, however, is almost never worn. Men may shave or not, as they please.

The ideas of right and wrong in Keene are drawn entirely from the *Bible*, although their interpretation by the Adventist Church is stricter than by most Christian sects. The Adventists hold that anything which defiles the body is sinful; thus the ban on such things as spices, including pepper.

So it has come to pass that Keene, even in the 1980s, remains a community that has been nicknamed "Spotless Town" by its neighbors. It is so upright that its citizens are said to have the highest credit rating in Texas and bill collectors are unknown in the community.

Adventists say that their way of life is a guarantee of longevity. Church statistics show, for example, that nonmeat-eaters average fifty percent fewer heart attacks and a seven-year-longer life expectancy than their carnivorous counterparts. Since Adventists neither smoke nor drink, many insurance companies are willing to give them greatly reduced rates on life policies.

In Keene, however, insurance salesmen meet a unique kind of buyer resistance. In Texas's bit of heaven on earth, most of the residents believe that the Lord sends death when He thinks it is right. To insure against an act of God is regarded as an impiety.

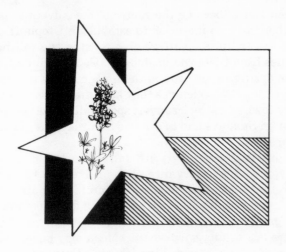

Texas A&M: Where Every Man Is On the Football Team

When Texas A&M University's football team takes the field, they might as well hang out a "Standing Room Only" sign in that section of the stadium reserved for students.

The seats are there, of course, but no self-respecting Aggie or his date will ever be seen sitting in one. From the arrival of the maroon-clad team on the field, through the warm-ups and pre-game ceremonies, everybody stands. They continue standing from the kickoff to the gun sounding the end of the game.

First-time spectators at a Texas A&M football game often marvel at this unique display of spirit on the part of the student body. If they listen closely, however, they'll soon get a musical explanation from the students of why it's a long tradition for them to stand through every game. The cheerleaders suddenly will call "Twelfth Man!" to the rows of fans, the Aggie band will sound off and the students will sing:

> "Texas Aggies down in Aggieland,
> We've got Aggie spirit to a man.
> Stand united, that's the Aggie theme,
> We're the Twelfth Man on the team."

Down on the playing field, the coach knows that the students mean what they say. The whole Cadet Corps, the men who are civilian students and even the women, now that Aggieland is coeducational, stand so anyone of them can rush

E. King Gill never got into the game, but he was the original "12th man" that started a great football tradition at Texas A&M University.
—Courtesy of Texas A&M University

down to the field if the coach needs them to play. It isn't likely to happen, of course, since there are some two score substitute players already suited up and sitting on the bench. But it almost happened once upon a time and that's how the Twelfth Man tradition was born.

Unlike most other Aggie traditions, this one didn't begin on the team's home turf, Kyle Field, on the College Station campus. It started in the old Fair Park Stadium in Dallas on a cool, windy January 2, 1922. The occasion was the first Dixie Classic, forerunner of the Cotton Bowl and the other football extravaganzas now played on New Year's Day. The visiting team was Charlie Moran's Praying Colonels of Centre College, one of the nation's best. Defending the honor of the Southwest Conference were the Texas Aggies coached by a thirty-one-year-old youngster named Dana Xenophon Bible.

In the stands that day was an Aggie cadet named E. King Gill, a sophomore who played both basketball and baseball for A&M. He also had lettered in football as a freshman and had been used as a substitute back early in his sophomore year, but had quit the team to devote his time to baseball. On this day, he had planned to be nothing more than a spectator. Then Jinx Tucker, the late great sportswriter from Waco, asked Gill to join him in the press box and serve as his spotter.

Both Tucker and Cadet Gill harbored only the dimmest of hopes that the Aggies could beat the Colonels. Harvard, then one of the real football powers in the East, had lost to the team from Danville, Kentucky. The Colonels, almost as famous for their travels as they were for their prayers in the pre-game huddle, had knocked off competition all over the country. The week before, in San Diego, California, they had embarrassed a powerful Arizona team and they didn't plan to give the Aggies their last game of the season.

Although this was long before the newspaper wire services began their weekly ratings of college football teams, sports writers were unanimous in their opinion that Centre College probably had fielded a squad that was almost unbeatable. Quarterbacking the Colonels was Alvin (Bo) McMillin, named All-American by Walter Camp for three successive years. Red Roberts, the end who caught McMillin's passes, also was a three-time all-American. The center, Red Weaver, also carried the All-American accolade.

The Texas Aggies not only were smaller, but their ranks had been thinned by injuries. Coach Bible arrived at Fair Park with only seventeen players and the hope that they could survive the Centre dreadnaught.

In the first quarter, however, a lucky break came the Aggie's way when they were forced to punt. The Centre safety caught the ball on the run in his own end zone and the Aggies nailed him behind the goal line for a safety.

Texas A&M's two-point lead infuriated the Colonels. When they received the kickoff after the safety, McMillin led a steady power drive, aided by an occasional pass, that drove the Aggies steadily back. Then, on fourth down and the ball resting six inches away from the goal, McMillin took the ball and charged toward pay dirt. The Aggie line held and the great quarterback was stopped.

The goal line stand by the Aggies, however, was costly. During the Centre drive, Bugs Morris, the A&M quarterback, was knocked out. Team captain Heinie Weir, the halfback, got a broken leg. A third player was lost during the quarter. By the end of the half, Coach Bible had only twelve players left.

In the press box, Jinx Tucker turned to his spotter, E. King Gill. "If this keeps up, son, old D.X. is gonna call you."

Tucker wasn't kidding. Early in the third quarter, the Aggie's fumbled deep in their own territory. On the next play, Centre ran the ball in for a score and kicked the extra point to take a 7-2 lead. They also added number six to the Aggie injury list leaving Sammy Sanders with a twisted knee. Now the entire squad — all eleven of them — were on the field. If there was one more injury, Bible could no longer field a complete team. Would he have to forfeit a game that already appeared lost?

The disconsolate coach rose slowly and looked up toward the press box. With one hand he motioned to Gill and pointed to the bench with the other. Gill rushed down the stands and jumped onto the field.

"King," Coach Bible greeted him, "it doesn't look like I'm going to have enough players to finish the game. You may have to go in there and stand around awhile."

Gill rushed under the stands (there were no team dressing rooms in the old Fair Park Stadium) and got into uniform. In moments he was back on the bench alongside Coach Bible. The

30

end of the game still was forty minutes away, but now Texas A&M had its "twelfth man" — its lone substitute if there was another injury. Gill, despite the fact that he had turned in his uniform early in the season and wasn't even sure that he remembered the plays, was ready to try. That was all that Bible could ask.

The coach's gesture of desperation went almost unnoticed by the crowd in the stadium that day. There was no cheer when Gill suddenly appeared to take his place on the bench. Even the press box crowd, usually alert for human interest stories, virtually ignored Bible's desperate move. In reporting the game, only two newspapers even mentioned that E. King Gill, a substitute player, had been called from the stands to be ready if needed.

However, the appearance of the twelfth man on the bench put new fire into the Aggies remaining on the field. Whether inspired by Gill's presence or the overconfidence of the Centre team, they made two first downs in quick succession. Then Louie Miller, a substitute halfback, gobbled up four yards on a swing around right end. On the next play, Miller started around end again, then stopped suddenly and lofted a pass to Jack Evans. He sprinted untouched for thirty yards and scored.

In recapturing the lead, the Aggies also took command of the game. Puny Wilson scored on another thirty-yard sprint. They scored still another when Bo McMillin, Centre's touted All-American quarterback, was rattled by the Aggie's rush and chunked an errant pass into the arms of Ted Winn. He dashed forty yards for another Aggie touchdown.

Centre finally managed to score again in the fourth quarter, but one of the surprising upsets in all of the history of football was in the making. The final score read: Texas A&M 22, Centre College 14. And E. King Gill, who had come down from the stands to be the twelfth man if needed, still sat quietly on the bench.

A unique tradition was born that day, however, and it remains one of the many memorable contributions that Dana X. Bible made to the great game of football. Bible, now deceased, retired from his last coaching post at The University of Texas, A&M's arch rival. However, he always remembered that blustery day in Fair Park Stadium as one of the most exciting in his illustrious career.

Like many other traditions, however, it was a long time in catching on. Aggie coaches and students soon forgot the incident and, for more than a decade, behaved like football fans everywhere — standing only when something exciting was happening on the field. Then, in the 1930s, a sports writer dug out the story of E. King Gill's being drafted as the "twelfth man" and a new era in school spirit was born.

Today every Aggie student, coeds included, stand through every game, waiting to be called to the field of play in case they are needed.

The Last
"War Between the States"

In 1931, the sovereign states of Texas and Oklahoma went to "war."

Fortunately for the Texas forces, the nine-day affair was bloodless and shotless because the military odds they faced were even greater than those with which the Alamo defenders met almost a century before. In the argument with Oklahoma, the entire fighting force of the Lone Star State consisted of six Texas Rangers, plus the Grayson County sheriff and his four deputies. Their only arms were Colt .45 revolvers.

By all odds, Oklahoma had the superior fighting strength. Lacking a force like the Texas Rangers and unwilling to leave the matter in the hands of its Bryan County sheriff, Oklahoma sent five companies of its best National Guards to the site. Their arms included a machine gun platoon and a howitzer.

The two "armies," each with a separate objective, dug in on opposite banks of the Red River, the boundary between the two states. The Texas Rangers had one assignment: To keep traffic on U.S. Highway 75 from using a new free bridge that had been built across the river. The objective of the Oklahoma Guard was similar: To prevent traffic from entering the Sooner State over a Texas-owned toll bridge that stood a few hundred yards downriver from the new span.

The net result of the fight was that traffic on the heavily traveled highway that stretches from Galveston to Winnepeg,

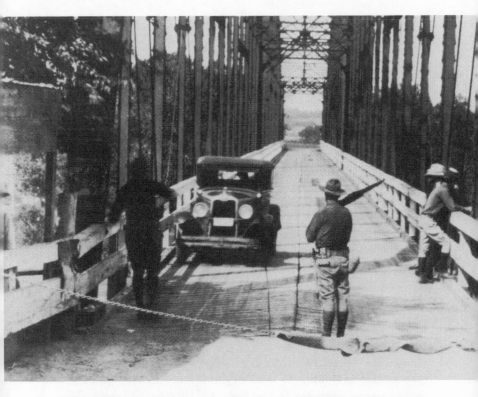

While Oklahoma National Guardsmen closed the toll bridge linking that state and Texas, the new Red River free bridge was blocked by Texas Rangers. The incident almost started a "war" between the two states in 1931.

—Photo by Claud Easterly, The Denison *Herald*

Canada, came to a grinding halt. It remained so until the opposing "armies," the governors of the two states and the Federal courts got the bridges open. However, the basic point at issue —whether individuals have the right to build bridges across streams and charge the public for their use —has never been satisfactorily settled.

Highway commissions of both Texas and Oklahoma precipitated the Red River War several years before when they decided to free all toll bridges crossing the stream. Their plan was simply to purchase the toll bridges from their owners. Stockholders of three of the bridge companies — those owning spans between Gainesville, Texas, and Marietta, Oklahoma; Ringgold, Texas, and Terral, Oklahoma; and Denison, Texas, and Colbert, Oklahoma — refused to sell. The two Highway Commissions then agreed to build new free bridges at these points and thus force the toll span owners out of business.

As was expected, the toll bridge owners filed a lawsuit hoping to prevent the states from building the free spans. When they lost in the courts, the owners of the Denison–Colbert bridge decided they would sell it. Their asking price was $60,000, payable when the parallel free bridge was completed. As a part of the sales agreement, they asked for the right to increase tolls until the free bridge opened. If the new span was completed short of fourteen months, Texas also would have to pay the toll owners $10,000 for each month in which they had not been able to charge motorists.

Texas was agreeable. However, the U.S. Defense Department (War Department in those days) has control of all navigable streams. The Federal government denied the request for the increased tolls.

In January, 1931, as the new bridge neared completion, the owners of the Denison-Colbert toll span went to court again. They demanded $60,000 from the Texas Highway Commission as payment for their bridge plus an additional $30,000 they claimed that they had lost in tolls after the War Department refused their request for an increase. Federal Judge T.M. Kennerly, sitting at Houston, granted the toll owners an injunction which prohibited the opening of the free bridge to traffic. At his orders, barricades were placed across the entrance to the structure on the Texas approach.

In Oklahoma City, Governor William H. "Alfalfa Bill"

Murray didn't like Judge Kennerly's decision and said so. He had promised the people of Oklahoma that all Red River crossings would be toll free. He intended to keep that promise.

By July 16, 1931, his temper had reached the boiling point. That afternoon, three Oklahoma Highway Department employees, acting on the personal orders of Governor Murray, drove up the north approach to the span, crossed it and kicked aside the Texas barricades.

For the next few hours, the traffic jam was broken and hundreds of cars poured across the new free bridge in both directions. But in Austin, Governor Ross S. Sterling had no intention of letting this affront to Texas pass. He sent Texas Rangers to Denison to reconstruct the barricades and to enforce the blockade with a round-the-clock guard.

Again it was Governor Murray's move. He countered by ordering four companies of infantry and a howitzer company of Oklahoma National Guards to the scene. Barred from opening the free bridge again except by risking a confrontation with the Texas Rangers, the guardsmen tried a different offense. They plowed up the highway leading to the Oklahoma approach to the toll bridge. This action effectively closed all traffic across the river at this crossing.

For three days, the bloodless battle continued with neither side giving in. Then Governor Murray heard that traffic was being detoured over another toll bridge six miles down river owned by the Kansas, Oklahoma & Gulf Railroad. He promptly sent a contingent of guardsmen to plow up the road leading to that span, too.

Under Governor Murray's strict martial law, the bridges were to be defended "against all authority except the President of the United States." He dared the courts to take any action against his blockade of the highways leading to the toll bridges.

Governor Murray, who admitted that he liked a good fight, made a field inspection trip to the battlefield and set up his own GHQ in a tent on the site. Governor Sterling continued to direct operations from the safety of Austin.

Meanwhile, the Oklahoma Guard dug in on the north bank of the river and protected its position by putting its howitzers and machine guns in place. The only shooting went on in the Texas Ranger encampment, however. The Rangers amused themselves by splitting playing cards and striking matches at twenty paces by firing their revolvers. The only "casualty" of the war came when an Oklahoma infantryman fell and ran his bayonet through his leg.

This event caused a momentary truce as Rangers helped carry him across the bridge to the Texas side and then rushed him four miles to Denison, the nearest hospital.

Finally, on July 25, Judge Kennerly, whose injunction had caused it all, made an "armistice" possible. He dissolved the injunction and permitted Texas to remove the barricades that closed the highway approach. One of the first cars across the free bridge was a black limousine carrying the triumphant governor of Oklahoma.

Once the barricades were down, the Texas Rangers went home. The Oklahoma Guard refused to leave, however, because Judge Kennerly hadn't decided whether or not he would make the dissolution of the injunction permanent. This he did on August 6 and the Guard went back to their workaday jobs in Oklahoma. The Red River bridge was forever free of tolls and the "war" was over.

However, the fight was not. It was to go on in the courts where the toll bridge owners still sought payment for their losses. Eventually they negotiated a new contract with Texas whereby the state would pay them a total of $165,000, but that later was repudiated. They also won a $168,000 judgment against the state of Oklahoma, but that also was reversed later by a Federal Appeals Court. Finally, in 1938, peace at last was assured in the war of the bridges when Texas handed over $50,000 for full title to the toll span. Oklahoma also agreed to a settlement but never paid off.

Today both the free bridge that caused the "war" and the old toll span (now also free) are still in use. U.S. Highway 75, now four lanes, required the building of still another span across the river to accommodate the traffic. So three bridges now cross the river at that point.

In the almost half a century since, the wounds of the bridge war have healed and Texans and Oklahomans have all but forgotten the fight. They were reminded of it again in the Second World War, however, when Hitler used the incident for propaganda purposes. The Nazi propagandists circulated pictures of the Oklahoma National Guard massed against the Texas Rangers and many German newspapers printed them as "proof that internal dissension exists in the U.S.!"

Texans and Oklahomans, using their common free bridge for neighborly visits across the Red River, heard about the pictures and smiled.

The Great Spaceship Hoax
—Or Was It?

Did an interterrestrial vehicle, cigar-shaped and blazing with lights, whiz into the North Central Texas town of Aurora on an April dawn in 1897, circle the public square and then crash into a farmer's windmill and explode?

It's a question that dozens of scientists, uncounted UFO buffs and an army of journalists haven't been able to answer. After years of countless investigations, nobody is willing to say with certainty that the Aurora spaceship story either is fact or else is the hoax of the century. There are arguments to support both theories.

Whatever happened — or didn't happen — at daybreak in a Wise County village thirty miles northwest of Fort Worth had its beginning several days before when newspapers in the West and Middle West began reporting sightings of a mysterious airship in the skies. It was spotted in Moline, Illinois, Iowa, in Wisconsin and in half a dozen Indiana communities before it was first reported in Texas on April 14 when it was seen over Denton.

In the days that followed it was spotted over Weatherford and Corsicana. In Fort Worth at least two reputable witnesses said they had watched it land in the city's park. From Stephenville, the editor of the newspaper there said the craft hovered so low over the town that he was able to shout a request to the pilot for an interview. The invitation was declined.

Joseph E. (Truthful) Skully, a brakeman on a Texas and Pacific Railway freight train, claimed to have had a close-up of the pilot. Skully, whose reputation for veracity won him his unusual nickname from fellow railroaders, reported that he saw the ship sitting in a clearing on the ground when his train stopped to take on water at Hawkins, in Wood County. He said the pilot, whom he described as "tall and spare," was making repairs to one end of the craft.

The spaceship, if such it was, must have been capable of tremendous speed. On the same day that it was supposedly promenading around East Texas, the *Rocky Mountain News* reported that it had been seen over Denver, Colorado. Not only that, but the craft had dropped a tiny parachute made of tissue paper and string to which was attached this message:

"This is dropped in hope that someone will find the note. We are in an airship but are lost."

The SOS was so authentic that the Army Signal Service in Denver considered sending its one hot air balloon into the wild blue yonder to search for the ship. This action was not taken, probably because earth creatures knew that no such lighter-than-air machine existed. After all, this was 1897 — six years before the brothers Orville and Wilbur Wright got their airplane off the ground at Kitty Hawk, North Carolina.

Meanwhile the publicity about the stogie-shaped airship sightings continued. Even *Harper's Weekly*, that much respected national magazine, reported the story in three consecutive issues. So it wasn't surprising that Texans breathed easier when they read the following story on April 19, 1897, on page 5 of *The Dallas Morning News:*

AURORA, Wise Co., Tex., April 17 — About 6 o'clock this morning the early risers of Aurora were astonished at the sudden appearance of the airship which has been sailing through the country.

It was traveling due north, and much nearer the earth than ever before. Evidently some of the machinery was out of order, for it was making a speed of only ten or twelve miles an hour and gradually settling toward the earth. It sailed directly over the public square, and when it reached the north part of town, collided with the tower of Judge Proctor's windmill and went to pieces with a terrific explosion, scattering debris over several acres, wrecking the windmill and water tank and destroying the judge's flower garden.

T.J. Weems, the U.S. Signal Service officer at this place and authority on astronomy, gives it as his opinion that he (the pilot) was a native of the planet Mars.

Papers found on his person — evidently the record of his travels — are written in some unknown hieroglyphics and cannot be deciphered.

The ship was too badly wrecked to form any conclusion as to its construction or motive power. It was built of some unknown metal, resembling somewhat a mixture of aluminum and silver.

The story, signed S.E. Haydon, went on to say that the pilot would be buried at noon the next day in the Aurora Cemetery.

The story of the crash was not copied by other newspapers in Texas or elsewhere. This may explain why reports from other areas of sightings of the craft continued to appear for a few days. Within a week, however, the newspapers had returned to reporting on U.S. troubles with Cuba and the Greek–Turkish War and the strange spaceship was all but forgotten.

In Aurora, a body was placed in a grave in the community cemetery after a Christian burial. It was marked, according to legend, with a stone on which was carved the Greek letter Delta with some circles inside. Until a few years ago, such a stone did mark a grave in the Aurora cemetery but it has since disappeared.

After a few weeks, the incident was all but forgotten and no attempt was made by scientists or the press to substantiate the story. In fact, the story of the Aurora airship was ignored for almost seven decades. Then, in 1966, a British magazine published for flying saucer fans heard about the supposed crash and sent a writer to check it out. By that time, however, virtually all of the Aurora citizens who were alive in 1897 had died and the journalist turned up few facts that might verify the incident.

Another seven years passed before any serious investigation was made. In 1973, the Unidentified Flying Objects Bureau of Oklahoma City, a private organization funded by UFO buffs, sent a team to Aurora. They were joined by investigators from the Midwest UFO Network, a similar organization headquartered in Quincy, Illinois, and by the National Investigative Committee on Aerial Phenomena. Heading the latter group was Major Donald E. Keyhoe, generally regarded as the nation's foremost authority on interterrestrial travel.

Within hours, Aurora was back in the news. Reporters,

television crews, treasure hunters and the curious descended on the tiny community. In many ways, they hampered the serious investigation by the UFO experts, but in other ways they proved helpful.

The journalists turned up the fact that the "S.A. Haydon" who signed the story of the crash published in the *Dallas News* was actually F.E. Hayden, a prominent cotton buyer in the community and not a reporter at all. There is some reason to believe that he wrote the story in jest, hoping that the publicity would help the economy of the community.

The Judge Proctor, on whose land the spaceship supposedly crashed, really was the local justice of the peace. The T.J. Weems identified in the story as a U.S. Signal Service officer and authority on astronomy, was neither. He actually was the town blacksmith.

Some residents of Aurora contend, however, that the story was not a hoax; that the errors of fact in Hayden's newspaper account were honest mistakes. They point out that he wasn't a trained reporter and that he may have made Weems an "astronomer" in an attempt to give credibility to a story he knew the outside world would find hard to believe.

The results of the 1973 investigations seem to support this theory. Using the latest electronic equipment, the UFO experts found metal fragments at the crash site which were small, thin and jagged as if torn apart by an explosion. The pieces were brown on one side (all who reported seeing the spaceship agreed that it not only was shaped like a cigar but was the color of cured tobacco) and protected by a gray covering on the other. The experts were puzzled by the fact that the material could not be identified as any known metal.

The location of the crash, as described in Hayden's news story, was easily found by the investigators. The strange metal pieces they discovered were all found at that site and nowhere else. Most puzzling of all to the investigators is the fact, attested to by numerous old-time residents, that no vegetation of any kind has ever grown where the spaceship supposedly nosed into the ground. The soil, however, is rich and *was* the site of Judge Proctor's garden.

The electronic detection equipment used in the 1973 investigation also indicated that metal similar to the kind found at the crash scene is somewhere in the Aurora Cemetery. However, there are an estimated 125 unmarked graves in the burial ground and the stone that supposedly marked the last resting place of the spaceship's pilot disappeared long ago. To prevent the UFO investigators from disturbing any of the graves, members of the Aurora Cemetery Association set up all-night vigils at the property. The pilot's grave, if it exists, was never located.

Although no witnesses to the supposed spaceship crash were located in the 1973 investigation, several lifetime residents of Aurora told stories that their parents had told them of the incident. Their accounts seem to confirm the statements in Hayden's news story.

Did some kind of aircraft crash in the village of Aurora years before man learned to fly, or was the 1897 story a hoax? Even those most knowledgeable about UFOs can't say for sure. But they do insist that *something* exploded into Judge Proctor's windmill almost a century ago and it carried a human, an animal or maybe a humanoid to its death.

Perhaps one day we will know if a Texas town was the site of the world's first spaceship accident or only the scene of practical joke.

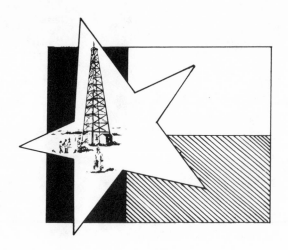

Clara Driscoll led the second battle for the Alamo and finally won it.
—From The San Antonio *Light* Collection of The Institute of Texan Cultures

The Battle of the Alamo
that History Forgot

The first battle of the Alamo — and the one remembered by history — lasted only thirteen days. The second battle lasted sixty-nine years and most history books don't even mention it.

General Antonio Lopez de Santa Anna and his Mexican legions annihilated Colonel William B. Travis and his 187 defenders of the old mission in a no-quarter battle that began on February 23, 1836. On March 6, the Alamo fell, leaving Travis and his men dead and the building in ruins.

The second battle of the Alamo really began the very next day. That was the fight to preserve this "cradle of Texas liberty" as a shrine for all time to come. This second conflict was to last almost seven decades, involve more Texans and, in some ways, was as fierce as the last stand Travis and his men made there. It also was a fight which a handful of dedicated Texans almost lost, but not quite.

The Alamo had, in fact, been something of an unwanted derelict almost since its founding in 1718 as the Mission San Antonio de Valero. In 1744 construction finally began on its famous chapel. However, five years after it was completed in 1757, the twin towers collapsed, leaving the church without a roof and filled with debris.

By 1783, disastrous epidemics had killed off so many of the Indians that the mission was abandoned and became an ordinary village pueblo. Ten years later its archives were moved to San Fernando Church in the village across the San Antonio River. In 1803, a company of Spanish soldiers from Alamo del

Parras, in northern Mexico, was sent to San Antonio and stationed at the old mission. They were homesick for Alamo and gave the name to the Mission Valero.

By the time of Santa Anna's renowned siege, the mission property was in disrepair and was anything but a military prize. Its thick outer walls, nine to twelve feet high, did, however, offer Travis and his men the best fortifications available and he elected to make his stand against the Mexicans there. In so doing, he made the Alamo one of the most famous buildings in all of history.

It was not so regarded after the battle of 1836, however. For five years, nothing much happened to the Alamo except that what was left of the chapel and walls continued to deteriorate. Then, in 1841, the Republic of Texas gave the Alamo and the other mission churches back to the Roman Catholic Church. The Church, in turn, leased the property to the U.S. government and, in 1849, it became a quartermaster and commissar depot for the Army. It remained that way until 1861, when the Confederates took it over. In 1865, when the Civil War ended, the federal government took control again.

In 1877, the Catholic Church sold the convent portion to a San Antonio man who did some additional renovation. In 1886 the convent was sold again and converted into a wholesale grocery warehouse. It later served as a wholesale liquor establishment. Meanwhile the State of Texas, concerned at what was happening to the Alamo, bought the chapel portion back from the Catholic Church and gave it to the City of San Antonio to care for.

This was the situation in 1891 when the second battle of the Alamo began in earnest. In that year, an organization known as the Daughters of the Republic of Texas came into existence with the organization of chapters in Galveston and Houston. Within a year, two other chapters were formed — one in Austin named for Colonel William B. Travis and a second in San Antonio named for Lorenzo De Zavala, first vice president of the Texas Republic. It was the women who led these two chapters who became the principal combatants in the fight.

Heading the San Antonio chapter was Miss Adina De Zavala, granddaughter of Lorenzo, and an early leader in efforts to preserve the Alamo. In 1892 she had obtained a verbal promise from the private owners that they would not sell the

46

convent portion without giving her organization the opportunity to acquire it. By 1902, she was on the Executive Committee of the Daughters and had put through a resolution urging the State of Texas to buy back all of the missions (including the Alamo) and place them under the control of the DRT.

Meanwhile, Clara Driscoll of Corpus Christi, daughter of a wealthy ranching family, also had expressed interest in making the Alamo a shrine. Between frequent trips to Europe, she wrote letters to Texas newspapers urging that private funds be raised to protect and preserve the shrine. In 1903, she came home to Texas, joined the De Zavala chapter of the Daughters and began to devote herself seriously to the project.

When the property adjoining the state-owned Alamo chapel was offered for sale and the Daughters of the Republic were unable to come up with the $75,000 asking price, Clara Driscoll began negotiations with the owners. In 1904, after the Daughters had raised only $7,000 toward the purchase, Miss Driscoll put up the money and took title to the property. To her the convent section was not important since it had been renovated since the 1836 battle. Her hope was to tear it down and turn the area into a park.

Miss De Zavala, however, disagreed with this view. She contended that the major struggle had been in the convent and monastery and that this was the portion of the complex to be saved and restored. Thus surfaced the first signs of disagreement between Miss Driscoll and Miss De Zavala. More was to come as the second battle of the Alamo slowly began to build.

In 1905, Miss Driscoll turned the Alamo property over to the state in exchange for $65,000 in warrants. About the same time, the De Zavala chapter of the Daughters not only asked the state to deed the property to their organization, but to make the San Antonio chapter the custodian. Miss Driscoll retaliated by asking the state DRT president to give her temporary control of the Alamo until a meeting of the Executive Committee of the Daughters could be held. Miss Driscoll was given custody of the property and left a representative in charge while she went off for a long stay in New York.

Miss Driscoll's train had hardly reached New York before Miss De Zavala had talked the City of San Antonio into releasing the keys and the custody of the Alamo to her. On November 3, 1905, the DRT filed suit against Miss De Zavala stating that she had taken illegal possession of the church and asking the court to force her to release control of the property.

Miss De Zavala denied all allegations in answering the suit, but did surrender the property. Then Miss Driscoll and a number of her supporters resigned from the De Zavala chapter of the DRT and formed their own in April, 1906. This served to split the Daughters of the Republic into two warring factions which eventually led to Clara Driscoll's resignation from the organization in November, 1906. At the same meeting, the De Zavala chapter of the DRT was given custody of the Alamo property. Miss De Zavala and her supporters not only had won the custodianship they wanted but they were also in firm control of the executive committee of the Daughters. Or so they believed.

However, when that committee met the following May in Houston, it nullified much of the previous action of the anti-Driscoll majority and placed the custody of the Alamo in the hands of the general association, not the De Zavala chapter. Suddenly the sparring between the forces led by the Misses De Zavala and Driscoll had become a civil war within the DRT.

In June, 1906, the fight began in public when St. Louis interests bought property adjoining the Alamo and announced plans to build a hotel. Before spending $500,000 on the project, however, they wanted assurance that the Alamo property be cleared first of everything except the south wall of the old mission. That, they contended, was the only part of the original Alamo standing at the time of the battle.

At this point, most of Texas entered the fray. The state was divided into two camps —one favoring preservation of not only the Alamo chapel, but also all the remaining walls and buildings. The other side wanted the hotel built. Within the DRT, the Driscoll-controlled Executive Committee agreed to remove the buildings that had been occupied by the wholesale grocery in exchange for an agreement by the hotel people to build a park around the remaining chapel, pay for the park's upkeep and meet other considerations. The De Zavala group opposed that action.

Later the two factions went to court again, this time to determine which represented the legally constituted Daughters of the Republic of Texas. The Driscoll followers won this fight, but Miss De Zavala wasn't through. Early in 1908, she barricaded herself inside the old convent portion after the hotel proposal had fallen through and the DRT leadership had announced plans to rent this section to a San Antonio business.

Miss De Zavala's act in remaining on the property despite the fact that sheriff's deputies were posted to deny her both food and water attracted national headlines. More days in court followed and, on March 10, 1910, the Driscoll group of the DRT finally took formal control of the Alamo. The battle, however, was not over. In 1911, the Legislature appropriated $5,000 for the improvement of the Alamo and vested in Governor O.B. Colquitt the right to spend it.

In 1912, the restoration began with the removal of all of the old convent building except the west and south walls. (The DRT claimed that the remaining walls were not a part of the original convent, although other historians believe that they were.) Based on 1849 plans the U.S. government had used in its restoration of the building into a quartermaster's depot, the first story of the east wall was rebuilt. Then the money ran out. When Governor Colquitt asked for a deficiency appropriation to complete the work, the DRT went to court and got an injunction to stop him. From the beginning, the organization had fought Colquitt's interference.

Thus ended the second battle of the Alamo. The Daughters of the Republic of Texas forces led by Clara Driscoll had won not only in the courts but in public opinion as well. Even a Governor of Texas had entered the fight and lost.

Clara Driscoll died in 1945 in Corpus Christi, but her body was brought to San Antonio for the funeral and she lay in state in the Alamo, the shrine she had fought so hard and spent so much of her own money to preserve. Miss De Zavala, who continued to fight the rest of her life for the restoration of the Alamo's convent, died in 1955 one day before Texas celebrated its independence.

The second battle had lasted two thirds of a century, and more. But unlike the first, when the Alamo was lost, it had been saved as a shrine visited now by people from all over the world.

The Boom Town that Lived
Only One Day

You won't find Crush, Texas, on any map or in the U.S. Postal Guide. But in the Lone Star State, where boom towns are as common as horned toads, Crush has a special place in history.

It was born on a September dawn in 1896 when a special train began disgorging its passengers at a brand new siding in a cow pasture not far from Waco. By noon it was a bustling city of 50,000, with a dozen lemonade stands (the precinct was dry), a restaurant, a midway with a carnival and even a jail. By nightfall, it was silent and deserted — a "ghost town" on the Texas prairie.

Unlike most boom towns, Crush had neither oil nor precious metal to lure the adventurous and keep them. It was born, became a city and then disappeared in a single day because of a train wreck — the first and only one of its kind in the history of Texas railroads.

Call it a stunt, a surprise or "locomotives at 100 paces," it is the most memorable example from the flamboyant era of publicity shenanigans. Today twice as many people may gather in the heat of a Texas summer for a Willie Nelson "birthday party" and twenty-four hours of continuous country western music. But the only attraction offered at Crush was a planned head-on collision between two trains — and the whole show lasted less than ten minutes.

A staged train wreck for the purpose of selling railway excursion tickets was the brainchild of W.G. Crush, general passenger agent for the *Katy* Railroad. The idea came to him one day in the 1890s as he traveled from New York to St. Louis. The boiler of the locomotive pulling his train exploded, wrecking the train at a desolate spot. Although there was no town nearby and communications and travel were slow, hundreds of the curious were on the scene within an hour.

"If this many people will come to see a wreck after it has happened," Crush asked himself, "what wouldn't they do to see a railroad collision that had been deliberately planned?" And so he proceeded to plan the biggest public train wreck ever staged anywhere.

If William George Crush were alive today, it is certain that he would be leading this state's current campaign to "See Texas first!" Crush, a Yankee who moved to Texas as a young man and spent most of his life in Dallas, believed that it took a special brand of showmanship to sell the Lone Star State. He used his own unique, and often spectacular, brand so successfully that he soon had Texans traveling everywhere in their own state and hordes of tourists from the North and East traveling to Texas for all kinds of special events.

Crush fathered and made a reality the greatest railroad excursion that ever operated into Galveston and did much to make that city's national reputation as a resort and recreation center. He was a leader in putting San Antonio's Battle of Flowers on the map. His advertising and promotional genius helped to make the State Fair of Texas in Dallas the nation's largest and best.

It was his planned collision of two speeding trains, however, and the one-day boom town he created as the site for the event, that gave Crush his lasting niche in the history of Texas.

September 15, 1896, was the date selected. He picked a wide valley sixteen miles north of Waco, not far from the town of West, as the site. Railroad crews cleared and mowed the pasturelands alongside the *Katy*'s main line and 500 track-layers were sent in to install the two-mile-long siding where the collision was to occur.

Crush then proceeded to run full-page advertisements in newspapers throughout the U.S. inviting one and all to the spectacle—and to ride one of the special trains of the *Katy*, of course.

As people rushed to railroad ticket offices to buy excursion tickets to the big wreck, plans moved forward to care for the crowds. Eight tank cars, connected with an eighth of a mile of pipe, were sent in to provide free water. Ringling Brothers and Barnum & Bailey Circus were prevailed upon to rent their big top for the restaurant that would serve only one meal.

Smaller tents were rented from the circus ostensibly to dispense lemonade in the dry precinct. However, concessionnaires ignored this legal technicality. When customers inquired what was being served, the answer was "hop ale and so forth." The "hop ale" was the code name for beer and the "so forth" was bourbon whiskey.

By 10 a.m. on September 15, 10,000 people were on hand and special trains were arriving at twelve-minute intervals. In all, thirty special trains arrived at the site and thousands more came by horse and buggy, spring wagon and on foot. Railroad records show that about 30,000 came on the *Katy* special trains, but the crowd was estimated at close to 50,000.

Two thirty-five-ton locomotives, surplus motive power which the *Katy* had planned to scrap, were used to stage the wreck. At the railroad's Denison shops, the old engines had been reconditioned. One was repainted a bright green, trimmed in red, and numbered *999*. The other was painted a bright red, trimmed in green, and given the number *1001*. Each locomotive pulled a string of six empty stock cars covered with canvas and painted to advertise the Texas State Fair and the Ringling Brothers circus.

For three days before the wreck, the crews made practice runs, timing each engine to make the run in exactly two minutes. On each locomotive, mechanics had installed a clamp against which the throttle could be opened and kept open. After the practice runs, each train could cover the one mile to the exact crash site in two minutes from a standing start.

At 5:10 p.m., the signal was given to the engineers to start. They eased the throttles forward, tied down the whistles and leaped out of their cabs. The two locomotives, rumbling like the gathering of a tornado, rapidly gained speed as they roared toward the collision point. A spontaneous cheer went up from the crowd, only to be drowned out as the flying monsters met with a splintering clang. The air was filled with flying missiles as the boilers burst, and one of the locomotive smokestacks sailed a quarter of a mile through the air, barely missing the crowd.

One man was killed by a flying brake chain and a woman died two days later from injuries received when a flying crosstie hit her. J.C. Deane, a Waco photographer covering the event for The Dallas *Morning News*, was struck in the eye by a flying bolt but recovered. At least a dozen others were rushed to Waco hospitals to have their injuries treated.

To most of the thousands gathered there that day, however, the wreck was a spectacle they would remember all of their lives. For the *Katy* Railroad, the aftermath was a rash of damage claims brought by the maimed and injured that took years to litigate in the courts. The railroad nevertheless acclaimed the whole affair as one of its most successful promotion stunts. General Passenger Agent Crush was given a raise and continued to promote traffic for the line for several more decades.

For the town of Crush, however, the great train wreck brought oblivion. By dusk, the special trains had departed, the dust of the collision had cleared away, the big tent was coming down and only two wreckers and their crews remained to get the railroad line cleared. Today not even an historical marker designates the site of Crush, Texas —the only town in the country that was founded, grew to a city of 50,000 and died in just one day.

Thomas Volney Munson, whose experiment with growing native Texas grapes near Denison, won him the French Legion of Honor when he saved that nation's wine industry.

The Taste of Texas
in French Wine

Frenchmen don't like to talk about it, and most connnoisseurs don't know it, but there's a flavor of Texas in every glass of French wine.

Whether it's a vintage burgundy or this year's Bordeaux doesn't matter. Wines from any of the vineyards in the south of France all trace their ancestry to vines that once grew in the sandy loam of the Red River Valley of Texas near Denison. It was the root stock from these hardy Texas grapes, plus the know-how of the horticulturist who developed them, that saved the French wine industry from bankruptcy and oblivion almost a century ago.

Thomas Volney Munson, the horticulturist, was no Johnny-come-lately to the science of grape production. A native of Illinois and the recipient of two degrees from the Kentucky State Agriculture College, Munson had started his career as a nurseryman in 1871 in Lexington, the Kentucky capital. In 1874, he moved to Lincoln, Nebraska, planning to establish vineyards there.

As a college student, Munson had decided that the grape was the "most beautiful, most wholesome and nutritious, most certain and most profitable fruit that could be grown." He had traveled 50,000 miles in forty states gathering specimens, studying soil and testing the quality of plants — travels that were to help to make him the world's greatest living expert on the grape. His goal was to prove some of his theories on grape culture in the vineyards he intended to develop in Nebraska.

Two years of grasshoppers and blizzards left Munson's tender grape plants withered and dying, however, and he decided to move south. Two of his brothers, Joseph T. and William B. Munson, had moved to the new North Texas railroad town of Denison and they invited T. V. to come down and look over the prospects of establishing a nursery in Grayson County. Munson visited Texas, decided the sandy soil and warmer winters were to his liking and announced: "I have found my grape paradise. Surely this is the place for experimentation with grapes."

In his travels before moving to Texas, Munson had observed that the cultivated grapes of Europe were not grown successfully in the United States except in California. He noted, however, that wild grapes were plentiful almost everywhere. His hope was to establish vineyards at Denison which would be devoted entirely to developing new, strong varieties of native grapes that could be put into commercial wine production.

Along the bluffs overlooking the Red River, and in the rocky ravines of Grayson County, Munson located a number of different wild grapes. He launched a program of crossbreeding and developing new plants. Within a few years, he was growing some 300 varieties of native Texas grapes in his vineyards. One of their outstanding characteristics was their resistance to phylloxera, a root disease that often destroyed entire vineyards.

Not long after Munson began his culture of native Texas grapes, this dreaded root disease attacked a vineyard in southern France. *Phylloxera* does not kill at once. First symptoms are an enlargement of the vine's root system. Next the roots rot, the leaves turn yellow and the plant dies. By the time Munson had arranged the most complete botanical groups of-grape genus ever compiled for display at the Columbian Exposition of 1893 in Chicago, phylloxera had spread throughout the vineyards of France and it appeared that the wine industry of that country was doomed.

French agricultural experts attending the Exposition heard of Munson's work. On the chance that the hardy varieties of Texas grapes which he had developed might save the French vineyards from phylloxera, they invited him to send root stock to France. There every vineyard eventually was grafted with root stock from Texas and the wine industry was miraculously saved.

A grateful French government sent its minister of agriculture, Pierre Viala, to Denison to confer on Munson that nation's highest accolade: the French Legion of Honor. The Texan was only the second American to receive it — Thomas Alva Edison had been the first.

Munson went on to become an internationally known horticulturist. His papers on grape culture, most of them published between 1880 and 1909, are still regarded as standards today. His book, *Foundations of American Grape Culture*, first published in 1909, has been reprinted in many languages and is still regarded as the "bible" of the business.

When Munson died in 1913, his son, Will V. Munson — one of his eleven children — carried on his father's work for a few years. And the family, in accordance with their illustrious father's last wish, erected over his grave in Denison's Oakwood Cemetery a granite shaft entwined with grapevine carved into the stone.

Later Will V. Munson gave the vineyards to Texas A&M University. For reasons never satisfactorily explained, the vines were later destroyed. Thus all of the original Munson vineyards disappeared —but not all of the varieties he developed.

Burleson Graham, an industrialist and grape fancier of La Grange, undertook to recover as many of the Munson varieties as possible. Mr. Graham and his associates had, at last count, something like fifty of these, varying from tiny rootings to bearing vines.

The Rare Plant Study Center at The University of Texas in Austin also became interested in helping to preserve as many of the Munson grapes as possible. Although they are not "rare" plants in the strict sense, they are regarded as "special." The University hopes that someday these vines, which carry the genes of some of the best of the Texas wild grapes, can be grown at Winedale, the historic stagecoach inn and farm at Round Top, Fayette County. This property was donated to The University by the late Ima Hogg and has been restored as one of the most authentic historic sites in the state.

Until Mr. Graham and others began the work of trying to recover the Munson varieties, the only known source was a vineyard in the North Texas county of Montague. Anthony Fenoglio, who died in 1972 at the age of eighty eight, was a friend and pupil of Munson. From the Munson varieties he grew, he provided cuttings to commercial wine producers in various parts of the country. Thus some California wines, along with those from France, trace their ancestry to Texas.

With wine-making reviving as an industry in Texas, there is a possibility that the superb grapes which Munson developed may once again be available to the world. Grayson County College, whose campus is just a few miles south of Munson's old home and vineyards, began a project in 1975 to recreate at least one-hundred varieties of the grapes which he developed. It is known as the T. V. Munson Memorial Vineyard and its work is supported by a foundation established by his decendants.

Five acres were set aside on the campus between Denison and Sherman. A greenhouse has been erected and a small museum built to honor the man for whom viticulturists in France and Yugoslavia long ago erected statues in his memory. Cuttings and vines are being made available to growers across the nation as a lasting toast to the Texan who long ago rescued the wine industry of France.

The Telegraph That Got Away

If President Mirabeau B. Lamar of the Republic of Texas, or Sam Houston, when he was governor of the state, had bothered to answer their mail, it's entirely possible that Texans today would pay few, if any taxes.

In 1838, Samuel F.B. Morse offered his new invention, the "electromagnetic telegraph," as gift to the new nation of Texas. He withdrew his offer more than twenty years later when no one bothered to write him a letter acknowledging it.

This strange episode in history began in Washington. Morse, a successful artist, had suffered a cruel disappointment. He had hoped to get a commission to do a painting for the nation's Capitol, but it went to another artist. Morse, seeking an antidote for this blow to his ego, turned to invention. Not long after, he developed his telegraph machine.

By 1838, Morse not only had a working model of the telegraph, but he had developed the code of dots and dashes that later would be used throughout the world. In that year, he decided the time had come to make a gift of the invention and he chose Texas as the recipient.

At the same time, he was trying vainly to persuade the United States Congress to build a telegraph line. However, it was not until 1843 that funds were appropriated for a line from Baltimore to Washington. It was then that Morse sent that first, famed message:

"What hath God wrought?"

His choice of Texas as the recipient of his gift of the telegraph undoubtedly grew out of his friendship with Memucan Hunt, minister to the United States from the young Republic.

Po'keepsie, August 9th 1860

May it please Your Excellency;

In the year 1838 I made an offer of gift of my invention of the Electro Magnetic Telegraph to Texas, Texas being then an independent Republic. Although the offer was made more than twenty years ago, Texas, neither while an independent State, nor since it has become one of the United States, has ever directly or impliedly accepted the offer. I am induced, therefore, to believe that in its condition as a gift it was of no value to the State, but on the contrary has rather been an embarrassment. In connection, however, with my other patent it has become for the public interest as well as my own that I should be able to make complete title to the whole invention in the United States.

I, therefore, now respectfully <u>withdraw the offer then made in 1838</u>, the better to be in a position to benefit Texas, as well as the other States of the Union....

To His Excellency
Sam. Houston
Governor of the State of Texas.

I am with respect and sincere personal esteem
Your obt. svt. Sam. F. B. Morse.

(TX)

When neither David G. Burnet nor Sam Houston answered his earlier letters, Samuel F. B. Morse wrote this one withdrawing his offer of his telegraph as a gift to Texas.

—Photo from the Archives Division, Texas State Library

60

From long conversations with Hunt, Morse knew that Texas was broke and looking for revenues from any reputable source. Apparently these conversations caused Morse to help the struggling new nation by giving his new invention to the government.

Hunt gratefully accepted the offer. It was not until April 27, 1839, however, that he wrote a letter to President Lamar and told him of Morse's generous gift. He told Lamar that he was putting the inventor's written offer in the "secret archives."

Hunt's archives must have been secret, indeed, because President Lamar apparently never saw Morse's official offer of the telegraph. At least, he never bothered to acknowledge it to the inventor. Hunt's covering letter to Lamar is in the State Archives in Austin, but no trace of Morse's offer of his invention has ever been found.

That the invention was never formally accepted by Texas is hard to explain in view of the state of the new nation's finances. After San Jacinto, the infant republic steadily went deeper into debt as it struggled with the problems that independence had brought. Imports exceeded exports and its balance of payments in the world trade market was deep in the red. In 1837, a U.S. bank panic had started a business depression that lasted through most of the lifetime of the Republic of Texas and added greatly to the fiscal problems of the new nation.

By the time annexation by the United States came in 1845, the public debt of the Republic had increased to $8 million and its paper money was virtually worthless. In fact, Texas didn't get out of debt until the Compromise of 1850 and the payment of $10 million to the state for relinquishing its claims to a large area to the north and west. Certainly it could have used every penny it might have gained from accepting Morse's invention.

Apparently Morse believed that Texas eventually would accept the gift. At least, he was a patient man. He continued to wait for some reply from Texas telling him that the electromagnetic telegraph was appreciated and accepted. He waited a total of twenty-two years, until after the Republic of Texas had become one of the United States. Still he never received even the courtesy of an acknowledgement.

Meanwhile, Morse and his associates were encountering

difficulties. Rival inventors had questioned Morse's rights to his patents on the telegraph and he had spent much time in the courts trying to protect them. In 1854, the U.S. Supreme Court finally upheld his patent rights. However, six more years passed before it occurred to Morse (or his lawyers) that he should formally withdraw his offer of the invention to Texas as a precaution against future litigation.

From Poughkeepsie, New York, on August 9, 1860, Morse dispatched a letter to Governor Sam Houston notifying him that the telegraph would no longer belong to Texas. The letter, also in the State Archives, reads as follows:

"May it please your Excellency:

"In the year 1838, I made an offer of a gift of my invention of the electromagnetic telegraph to Texas, Texas then being an independent republic. Although the offer was made more than twenty years ago, Texas, neither while an independent state nor since it has become one of the United States, has ever directly or impliedly accepted the offer.

"I am induced, therefore, to believe that in its condition as a gift it was of no value to the state, but on the contrary has been an embarrassment. In connection, however, with my patent, it has become for the public interest as well as my own that I should be able to make complete title to the whole invention in the United States.

"I, therefore, now respectfully withdraw the offer then made in 1838, the better to be in a position to benefit Texas as well as the other States of the Union."

Whether Governor Houston acknowledged this final letter from Morse isn't known. And why President Lamar and his successors ignored the offer of this generous gift may never be known. It probably got lost in the maze of red tape and bureaucracy that plagues even new nations.

For whatever reason Morse's gift was ignored, the fact remains that Texans today are still paying for the negligent way in which President Lamar handled his mail. Had the Republic of Texas accepted the telegraph, the world-wide royalties from the invention would, by 1916, have been large enough to pay all expenses of state government.

More than that, the continuing royalties would have by now created a permanent endowment fund of such size that Texans today would have had to pay few, if any, taxes.

Marshall, Texas
— "Capital" of Missouri?

Few Texans know it and most Missourians deny it, but the fact is that Marshall, Texas, once was the capital of the "Show Me" state.

Regrettably, the former Capitol and Executive Mansion of the state of Missouri no longer stand at the corner of South Bolivar and Crockett Streets in Marshall. They were torn down in 1951 before Texas became aware of the tourist value of such landmarks. But ninety years earlier, from the summer of 1861 until he died a year later, Governor Claiborne F. Jackson ran the government of the commonwealth of Missouri from the simple, one-story frame house that occupied a quiet residential street in Marshall.

Jackson, an acrimonious Southern sympathizer, was elected governor of Missouri on a Democratic ticket headed by Stephen A. Douglas. Like Douglas, Jackson had warned that if Abraham Lincoln were elected president, he would embroil the nation in a war between the states. Jackson feared that if war came, Missouri, a borderline state, might be invaded by Federal troops.

After his inauguration on January 3, 1861, Governor Jackson moved his government from Jefferson City to Boonville as a precaution. He placed Colonel John S. Marmaduke, who shared his Southern sentiments, in command of the state's troops and asked for 50,000 volunteers to bolster Missouri defenses.

A small force was recruited. However, on June 17, 1861,

This building, now demolished, once was the Capitol of Missouri for a time during the Civil War when that state's government moved to East Texas.

This was the home of Governor Claiborne F. Jackson in Marshall during the time he ran the government of Missouri from Texas.

Federal troops under General Nathaniel Lyon moved into Boonville, routed Colonel Marmaduke and his force and sent the Jackson government retreating south to Carthage. Another battle was fought at Carthage and Marmaduke managed to trounce the Union regulars. Jackson realized, however, that the odds were against them and he ordered the government moved to Texas.

With Lieutenant Governor Thomas C. Reynolds, the Secretary of State and a handful of other department heads, Governor Jackson left his troops behind and slowly moved his government southwest. He first set up his "capital" in Camden, Arkansas, moved on to Arkadelphia and then to Little Rock. Finally he picked the bustling port of Jefferson, then head of navigation on the Red River, as his Texas "capital."

Once his government arrived in Jefferson, however, Jackson learned that many of Missouri's wealthier citizens, most of whom sympathized with the Southern cause, had preceded him and established a colony in Marshall, then only a hamlet of 2,000. He decided to move on nineteen miles west to Marshall.

Judge Asa Willie, a member of the Supreme Court of Texas, had recently moved his family from Marshall to Austin for his term of office and Governor Jackson rented the Willie home as his seat of government. Across the street, at 190 East Crockett, stood the two-story, gabled home of Mrs. Mary Key, also unoccupied. It boasted inviting balconies, spacious lawns dotted with magnolia and wisteria and a porch of hotel proportions. He rented this home as his Executive Mansion.

Meanwhile, back in Missouri the Democratic Convention had met and repudiated Governor Jackson. In his place, the voters established Hamilton Gamble, a man whose feelings about the war were not so fractious and who liked the idea of keeping the government within the state.

Actually, Gamble was governor in name only. Jackson had thoughtfully taken the official state seal and all important records to Texas. Gamble had little to do except occupy the office.

Nevertheless Jackson resented the manner in which the Democrats had sought to remove him from an office given to him by the electorate. He decided to return to Missouri and get a firsthand report on what had happened. Leaving the Marshall government in charge of Lieutenant Governor Reynolds, Jackson returned to New Madrid, issued a proclamation from there declaring Missouri to be forever independent of the United States and called on the General Assembly to ratify it. The Assembly, the majority of which was loyal both to Jackson and the South, met in Neosho on October 21, 1861 and ratified the proclamation.

Satisfied that Missouri now was a free state, Jackson wrote Reynolds to continue running things from Marshall. The governor, however, wanted no part of running the government in exile. He headed for southern Arkansas and joined a fighting force of Southern secessionists. Reynolds officially assumed the title of governor and continued to run the state of Missouri from Marshall until Lee surrendered and the Confederacy collapsed.

Meanwhile, as the war grew in fury, more and more Missourians headed for their new "capital" in Texas. Perils and privations were beginning to stalk both the North and South, but this little town on the rich soil of East Texas was not touched by either. From a population of 2,000, Marshall tripled its size as more landowners moved in with their slaves.

Even today, the population of Marshall shows the effects of this period when it offered sanctuary. More than half of its present population of almost 25,000 are Negro — most of them descendants of the slaves brought in from Missouri and other states.

While Reynolds continued to administer the outlawed Missouri government, Governor Jackson's health failed. He died December 6, 1862, in an improvised hospital in Little Rock without ever knowing that the South would lose the war and that Missouri would return to the Union. Jackson's death did not deter Reynolds from carrying out his mandates and he kept the government going. Any hopes he may have had of some day heading an independent commonwealth died at Appomattox and he returned to Missouri after the war ended.

The capitol and official residence lived on in Marshall for another ninety years, however. In 1950, the one-time Governor's Mansion was offered for sale to any historically-minded benefactor who wanted to preserve it. When no buyer came forward, it was razed and replaced by a laundry.

A few months later, the owner of the old Missouri capitol offered it for sale on the same basis. Nobody wanted to buy the simple, one-story house that never had been a local tourist attraction. The citizens of Marshall had never erected any kind of a marker to remind passers-by that the unpainted clapboard structure once had been the official, but outlawed, seat of government of the commonwealth of Missouri. In 1951, the building was torn down.

Now there is an historical marker at the site which proclaims that Marshall, deep in the heart of East Texas, once was the capitol of the sovereign state of Missouri.

The Alamo Had a Coward, Too

Probably not one out of a thousand tourists who pause before the monument to the heroes of the Alamo on the State Capitol grounds in Austin knows it, but there is an embarrassing error among the names inscribed there. Along with Colonel William B. Travis, Jim Bowie and Davy Crockett is the name of one J.M. Rose.

There wasn't a J.M. Rose on the list of those who fought and died at the Alamo. But there was a Louis Rose. However, by the time the Mexican Army attacked on March 6, 1836, Louis Rose was not among those who defended the Alamo to the death. Three days earlier, Rose had elected to leave the other 182 defenders. His escape through enemy lines was successful, but he was destined to live out his life as a social outcast.

History, when it mentions him at all, remembers him as the only deserter at the Alamo.

On March 3, 1836, it was obvious that the Alamo was doomed and that its defenders would die. For ten days the mission had been under siege — ten days of hope for relief and assistance that hadn't come. On the morning of March 3, Colonel William Barret Travis, the commanding officer, called his men together, told them their situation was hopeless and offered any who wanted to leave the chance to escape. Then he drew a line in the dirt with his sword and asked those willing to stay to cross over it with him.

Tapley Holland was the first to respond and others followed one by one. Even old Jim Bowie, bedridden and desperately ill, asked that his cot be carried across the line. Finally every man had crossed the line except one.

Louis Rose, born in France in 1785 but a Texan by adoption, decided to try to save his life. Instead of crossing the line, he buried his face in his hands and fell prostrate on the ground. Tearfully he explained that he had so much sin on his soul that he was afraid to die without confessing to a priest.

Rose, known by the nickname, "Moses," was fifty-one and tired of war. As a teenager, he had fought with Napoleon's army and had shared the glories of conquest until the campaign to capture Moscow in 1812. Rose was with the French troops that were forced to retreat by the severe winter that cost thousands of lives. He was among the soldiers that did succeed in getting back safely to France and he remained a soldier through Napoleon's decline and exile.

Loyal to his ex-emperor, Rose became involved in a plot to restore Napoleon to power. When it failed, the plotters were expelled from France forever. Rose emigrated to the United States and made his way to Louisiana where he spent the first peaceful years since his boyhood.

At that time, Texas was still a part of Mexico but more and more Americans were coming in as settlers. With settlement came the desire for independence, but the few minor attempts at revolution were put down by the powerful Mexican Army. In 1826, however, one Hayden Edwards commanded a force that was able to take the town of Nacogdoches from the Mexicans. One of his soldiers was Moses Rose.

Rose liked Nacogdoches and decided to settle there. A dark, swarthy man who spoke Spanish fluently, he lived in the town's Mexican settlement. He got a job driving a freight wagon between Nacogdoches and Natchitoches, Louisiana, for Frost Thorne, a successful businessman. He also carried mail between the two communities.

The independence Edwards's revolutionaries had won for Nacogdoches was short-lived, of course, and the Mexican Army returned to power. Rose continued to work for Thorne but obviously didn't like the routine of a freighter. In 1832, when Colonel James Bowie took command of another revolutionary army, Rose joined. Bowie's force not only took Nacogdoches again, but drove the Mexican garrison out of town. Rose was among the twenty men Bowie handpicked to pursue the Mexicans and they succeeded in capturing the entire force of 310.

Rose fought with such distinction that he and Bowie became close friends. However, he again returned to civilian life. On May 8, 1834, his new employer, sawmill owner John Durst, gave him one hundred acres of land known as the Walker Ranch "in consideration of services rendered." It appeared that Rose would become a contented farmer.

In 1835, however, war between the Texians and Mexico again appeared imminent. Rose sold his farm and personal belongings and joined his old friend, Jim Bowie, in the march to San Antonio. They fought with General Edward Burleson's forces and succeeded in taking the town. Later Bowie was given command and he moved the remaining forces to a small mission on the edge of San Antonio de Bexar known as the Alamo.

General Santa Anna, furious because the rag-tag Texian Army had taken San Antonio, swore that he would obliterate the defenders in the Alamo. Thus began the siege that saw 182 men hold off an army of 5,000 superior troops for almost ten days while undergoing continuous bombardment and attack. It was to become one of the half dozen memorable battles in the history of the world.

Moses Rose, however, was to have no part of it. On the afternoon of March 3, he said goodbye to his friend, Bowie, climbed a wall of the Alamo and dropped his clothes into a puddle of congealed Mexican blood. Then he dropped over the side, made his way through the dead soldiers and Mexican pickets and eventually found safety.

In saving his life, however, he lost it. From that day forward, Louis "Moses" Rose was regarded as a traitor.

After weeks of hardship and travel by foot, he reached the home of an old friend, Abraham Zuber, at Iola, in Grimes County. Zuber was surprised to see Rose alive. On March 24, 1836, the *Telegraph and Texas Register*, official newspaper of the revolution published at San Felipe de Austin, had published a partial list of Alamo casualties. Rose was one of the seventeen listed as having died there.

or whom the least populated, but wealthiest, county in d.

—Courtesy of The Institute of Texan Cultures

Under questioning by the Zubers, Rose told the story of his cowardice and his escape. Later their son, William P. Zuber, himself a veteran of the fight for independence, was to tell the story in an article titled "An Escape from the Alamo" and published in *The Texas Almanac* in 1873.

Rose returned to Nacogdoches and tried to pick up the threads of his life. Having once been liked and respected by his fellow townspeople, he felt that they would understand his decision not to remain at the Alamo. They didn't, although Frost Thorne did give him a job at his lumberyard. Most of the residents regarded Rose with contempt and most wouldn't speak to him when they passed on the street.

In time, the feeling against Rose eased. However, three years after the fall of the Alamo, an incident occurred which demonstrated the contempt in which he would always be held. On July 17, 1837, he was called as a witness in a murder trial. In the court records, his name is spelled as "Luesa," the feminine version of Louis. Without doubt, the slur was deliberate — a reminder of his lack of courage in battle.

A year later, a Mexican tried to kill Rose on a Nacogdoches street. The Mexicans shared with the Texians a hatred of cowardice.

Tired of making a living at odd jobs, Rose opened a meat market in 1839 on Nacogdoches's Commerce Street. Customers came because he was the only butcher available, but there was little conversation. On two occasions, he threatened to kill customers who complained about the quality of the beef he sold.

When a competitor opened another market, Rose's business all but disappeared. Eventually he was forced to close his shop and become a cobbler in order to make a living. There were times when he was penniless and forced to borrow small sums in order to eat. Several notes still in the Texas Archives show that there were those who would lend money to the "coward of the Alamo" — but only at high rates of interest.

In 1842, Rose left Nacogdoches forever. He made his home on the farm of the Aaron Ferguson family who lived six and a half miles north of the town of Logansport in De Soto Parish, Louisiana. Today a street through the farm is known as Castoff Creek. Legend has it that it was named for Rose because he was a social castoff.

He died about 1850 and he may be buried in the Ferguson

family cemetery on the banks of Castoff Creek. Some historians believe that he is buried in East Texas near Mount Pleasant. For many years, a country cemetery between Alto and Rusk, in Cherokee County, had a soapstone marker bearing only the name "Moses Rose."

Nobody knows for sure the last resting place of the once brave soldier whom history remembers only as the coward of the Alamo.

Loving —
The Place with
The Most of the Leas

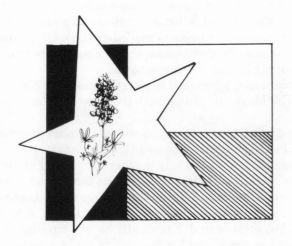

There is still one spot in this country other 220 million Americans have never wouldn't vacation there if all expenses we

It's a 647-square-mile chunk of Te County, and the chances of its ever becc for the jet set (or anybody else) are abc graphical location. In the first place, anywhere in the county; what little only cattle and a few sturdy old-ti ondly, there isn't an airport, a rai anywhere in the county and its o thirty miles of farm roads.

One of these, Farm Road 30 County has to the rest of Texas the county seat and only tow east in adjoining Winkler Cou Mentone for six miles and Reeves County, the only m northwest section of the co 652 provides a connectio the desolate southeaster

Mentone, which is idents, offers few ame boasts a gasoline st beer tavern. Howe Countians not a

Oliver Loving,
the U.S. is nam

physician, chiropractor, dentist or funeral home in the county, either. Neither is there a cemetery, nor is one needed. There has been only one recorded death in the county and it resulted from the only serious traffic accident ever reported there. The only two marked graves in the county are the final resting places of cowboys killed in range accidents years ago.

It has been almost fifty years since a birth was recorded in the county. However, residents seem to recall that a couple of babies may have been born some years ago in an oil field camp in the brush country, but nobody bothered to record the fact with the county clerk in Mentone.

Since 1970, when the U. S. Census officially declared Loving to be the most sparsely settled county, parish or borough in the country, residents have bragged that they have "the most of the least." At Keen's Cafe, owner Newt Keen will proudly recount the fact that Loving County, which has an abandoned church and no preacher, has an unusually moral population. The county has never had a serious crime reported in its precincts, has never had an arrest on a drug charge of any kind and the "vacancy" sign is almost always out on its one-cell jail.

However, even a long-time resident like Keen, who gave up ranch cooking to open Mentone's only social center (he dispenses beer), admits that Loving County might benefit from a few more conveniences. The county has no bank, has never had a movie theater and Mentone residents have to drive thirty-two miles to Kermit to pick up a loaf of bread because there is no grocery store. Except for Keen's emporium, the only other public recreational facility is the "state park" — a roadside rest stop west of Mentone where the traveler can pause to look at the deep ruts left years ago by Butterfield Trail stagecoaches.

Although Loving may be the least populated county in the U. S., it also is one of the wealthiest. In a given year, more than $70 million in black gold pours out of its oil and gas wells and petroleum activities in the county will drop close to $500,000 into the tax coffers. On the other hand, residents pay a total of about $2,000 a year in real estate taxes.

Some of this tax money once went to support the one school in the county, but that facility closed in 1978 for lack of students. Before it was closed, however, it gave Federal bureaucrats in Washington one of their biggest headaches. It started in 1972 when a U. S. court in Dallas instructed every Texas county that it had to participate in the government's Family Food Assistance Program for the poor. Loving County's judge fired off a curt letter:

"We don't need it, we don't want it and we can't use it if we're forced to take it."

Later the U. S. Department of Health, Education and Welfare notified the county that it had to integrate its schools. There were some red faces in Washington when word got back that the one school always had been open to all. Besides, there isn't a black in the entire county, although there are some Mexican-Americans.

When the government wanted to know what Loving County was doing about bussing, there was a ready answer. Since the Mentone school offered only the elementary grades, students in the upper levels had been bussed for years to Wink in an adjoining county.

Although Wink is only about thirty-five miles from Mentone as the crow flies, the school bus route is the longest in the nation. Because the county has almost no roads, the school bus has to travel to Orla, in Reeves County, then southeast by U. S. Highway 285 to a point where it intersects Farm Road 302. There it heads north to Wink. The round trip totals 154 miles!

Getting Loving's youngsters to Wink for their education (there were only seven between the ages of five and thirteen in the county in 1984) is not regarded by residents as a problem. Neither is the fact that out of the total population of ninety-one, only sixty-four are listed as able-bodied. Each of the latter is employed, thus giving Loving County the nation's only zero unemployment statistic. Residents boast that theirs is the only county in the nation where there has never been a welfare program of any kind and a food stamp has never been issued or redeemed.

Loving Countians trace much of their individual independence to that special breed of Texans who settled there in the mid-nineteenth century. One such was Oliver Loving, a legendary cattleman who came to Texas from Kentucky in 1845. In 1858, in partnership with John Durkee, he drove a herd of cattle from Palo Pinto County to Chicago, the first recorded incident of Texas cattle being driven directly to the slaughter house instead of to a shipping point like Abilene, Kansas.

Later he and another rancher, Charles Goodnight, established the famed Goodnight-Loving Trail from Texas to New Mexico.

In 1867, while en route over this trail with a herd bound for Fort Sumner, New Mexico, Loving and a companion were attacked by Indians. Loving, thinking himself fatally wounded, sent his companion ahead to warn Goodnight. Although Loving had been shot, scalped and left for dead, he crawled eighteen miles. He kept himself alive by chewing on an old leather glove. Rescued finally by a band of Mexican traders, he was taken to Fort Sumner. There he developed gangrene from his wounds and died. Before his death, however, he made Goodnight promise that he would bring his body back to Texas for burial. His wish was carried out and he is buried in Weatherford, Parker County.

Long before a county half the size of Rhode Island was carved out of Tom Green County and named for the stubborn rancher who refused to die until he was assured a Texas burial, the area had an early developer. He was another Kentuckian, John Pope, and he commanded a party of U. S. Army engineers who surveyed railroad routes through North Texas. Later he returned to search for water and a well bearing his name became a landmark on the Goodnight-Loving Trail. It's still known as Pope's Crossing on the Pecos River.

Pope's dream was to drill artesian wells along the Pecos and make the wasteland of what now is Loving County productive. He hauled drilling equipment from Indianola, on the Texas coast, to the area to try and prove that he could find water. He couldn't. Even today, oil drillers say they fail to find water in the county even at depths of 4,000 feet and more. As a result, residents still truck in their drinking water.

With no water and almost no population, organizing a government in the new county proved difficult. In 1893, a sheriff, county attorney and tax collector were named, but none qualified as a resident. By 1897, qualified people to hold the offices still hadn't been found and Loving was attached to Reeves County for the purposes of government. Then in 1925, oil was discovered and Loving County had a mild boom.

In 1931, residents again organized a government. Mentone, which was the only settlement, became the county seat. Within two or three years, the influx of oil drillers and suppliers had pushed the county's population to about 1,000. Most, however, didn't stay on once their work was finished. By 1940, despite the fact that oil was gushing from wells all over the county, population dwindled to 285. By 1950, it was down to 227 and has declined slowly since. The 1980 U. S. Census counted ninety-one people in the county, but residents say the actual permanent population is no more than eighty.

Most of the residents, whatever their actual number, don't feel that they are deprived. There is a kind of public library in the Mentone courthouse. Included is an 1892 edition of a book titled *Entertainment for Loving People*. Citizens enjoy reading the volume which arrived in a collection of surplus books from the Library of Congress years ago and deals with party games.

When Loving residents tire of the "library," they can go to Mentone's "art gallery" in the town's only gas station. The art resulted from a trip the late Frank X. Tolbert, a Dallas *Morning News* columnist and Texana authority, made to Europe in 1963. He stopped off in Menton, France, namesake of Loving County's seat. The mayor of the French city presented him with several beautiful paintings and photographs of Menton. Tolbert brought them back to Menton and they ended up in the gas station.

But that's Loving County, where the unusual is to be expected and where an art gallery in a gasoline station rates no special reaction from the citizenry. It's also a place where inconvenience and loneliness is a way of life. The nearest beauty shop or movie is at least thirty miles away and there has never been a newspaper or radio station in the county. It's a place where liquor has long been legal, but it's impossible to buy any. There was one place licensed to sell it years ago but it closed for lack of customers.

Even when the county had its lone school, there was no athletic program. There were never enough students to field two teams to play against each other.

But Loving Countians don't mind. They brag that they've got "the most of the least." And they don't smile when a rare tourist stops at the one cafe and beer emporium and repeats the old saw about Texas being the place with more cows and less milk, and where you can look farther and see less.

They don't smile, because, in Loving County, that's the truth.

Under questioning by the Zubers, Rose told the story of his cowardice and his escape. Later their son, William P. Zuber, himself a veteran of the fight for independence, was to tell the story in an article titled "An Escape from the Alamo" and published in *The Texas Almanac* in 1873.

Rose returned to Nacogdoches and tried to pick up the threads of his life. Having once been liked and respected by his fellow townspeople, he felt that they would understand his decision not to remain at the Alamo. They didn't, although Frost Thorne did give him a job at his lumberyard. Most of the residents regarded Rose with contempt and most wouldn't speak to him when they passed on the street.

In time, the feeling against Rose eased. However, three years after the fall of the Alamo, an incident occurred which demonstrated the contempt in which he would always be held. On July 17, 1837, he was called as a witness in a murder trial. In the court records, his name is spelled as "Luesa," the feminine version of Louis. Without doubt, the slur was deliberate — a reminder of his lack of courage in battle.

A year later, a Mexican tried to kill Rose on a Nacogdoches street. The Mexicans shared with the Texians a hatred of cowardice.

Tired of making a living at odd jobs, Rose opened a meat market in 1839 on Nacogdoches's Commerce Street. Customers came because he was the only butcher available, but there was little conversation. On two occasions, he threatened to kill customers who complained about the quality of the beef he sold.

When a competitor opened another market, Rose's business all but disappeared. Eventually he was forced to close his shop and become a cobbler in order to make a living. There were times when he was penniless and forced to borrow small sums in order to eat. Several notes still in the Texas Archives show that there were those who would lend money to the "coward of the Alamo" — but only at high rates of interest.

In 1842, Rose left Nacogdoches forever. He made his home on the farm of the Aaron Ferguson family who lived six and a half miles north of the town of Logansport in De Soto Parish, Louisiana. Today a street through the farm is known as Castoff Creek. Legend has it that it was named for Rose because he was a social castoff.

He died about 1850 and he may be buried in the Ferguson

family cemetery on the banks of Castoff Creek. Some historians believe that he is buried in East Texas near Mount Pleasant. For many years, a country cemetery between Alto and Rusk, in Cherokee County, had a soapstone marker bearing only the name "Moses Rose."

Nobody knows for sure the last resting place of the once brave soldier whom history remembers only as the coward of the Alamo.

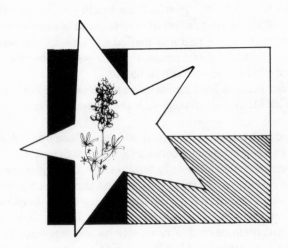

Loving —
The Place with
The Most of the Least

There is still one spot in this country which most of the other 220 million Americans have never seen and probably wouldn't vacation there if all expenses were paid.

It's a 647-square-mile chunk of Texas known as Loving County, and the chances of its ever becoming a watering place for the jet set (or anybody else) are about as remote as its geographical location. In the first place, there is no potable water anywhere in the county; what little there is tastes so bad that only cattle and a few sturdy old-timers can stomach it. Secondly, there isn't an airport, a railroad or even a bus station anywhere in the county and its only highways are fewer than thirty miles of farm roads.

One of these, Farm Road 302, is about the only access Loving County has to the rest of Texas and the world. It links Mentone, the county seat and only town, with Kermit, thirty-two miles east in adjoining Winkler County. Take the road southwest out of Mentone for six miles and it intersects U.S. Highway 285 in Reeves County, the only major thoroughfare in the area. In the northwest section of the county, another few miles of Farm Road 652 provides a connection to the north with a state highway in the desolate southeastern corner of New Mexico.

Mentone, which is home to about forty of the county's residents, offers few amenities. It is the site of the courthouse and boasts a gasoline station and a cafe which also doubles as a beer tavern. However, this lack of urbanity worries Loving Countians not a whit. There isn't a hotel, motel, drugstore,

73

Oliver Loving, for whom the least populated, but wealthiest, county in the U.S. is named.

—Courtesy of The Institute of Texan Cultures

Pancho Villa's War
To Make a Movie

Texas has been called "the Land of Odd." And why not? Where else in the world has a war been planned just to make a movie?

This wasn't a make-believe conflict staged on a studio set with professional actors, either. It was the real thing, and its star was Pancho Villa, bandit, murderer, revolutionary and — in 1914 — Mexico's Man of the Hour. He also was one of the most adroit press agents of his time.

Villa, like many another military leader, was vain. To conquer and rule wasn't enough to satisfy his super ego. He wanted his exploits recorded so that the world would never forget them, and the silver screen seemed to him to be the best possible medium. Only on motion picture film could his deeds of daring and valor be witnessed over and over again by generations still unborn.

His idea for staging a war for the benefit of the cameras was born when he and his army of peons were operating along the Texas-Mexico border. For relaxation, Villa used to slip into El Paso to enjoy what he called "moving movies" and he never forgot the way audiences responded to the images on the screen. He became convinced that audiences everywhere wanted to see Villa, the farmer elevated to *conquistador*, win his revolution. He also knew that there were Hollywood producers who would pay good *gringo* dollars for the right to film a powerful story — and Villa's war was realism at its best.

So it was that, on January 2, 1914, several of Villa's lieu-

Pancho Villa and his troops — the only army that ever fought a war in order to make a motion picture.

Courtesy Kuston Quality, El Paso (Used with permission)

tenants visited El Paso's "film row," an area where several motion picture companies had distribution offices. They informed several of the managers that General Villa was willing to sell the exclusive film rights to his war. He would be the star and his supporting cast would be the thousands of peons in his army.

Most of the film people scoffed at the idea. However, the El Paso manager of the Mutual Film Corporation wired his president, Harry E. Aitken, in New York. Aitken liked the idea of capturing the conquest of a country in live action and dispatched Frank M. Thayer, another Mutual executive, to El Paso to work out the details.

Thayer, based in Hollywood, got to El Paso on the fastest train out of Los Angeles. On Saturday, January 3, he met with Villa in an El Paso hotel room.

"We'll give you $25,000 and a percentage of the film's profits," Thayer told him. "However, there is one stipulation: You must fight your battles between 9 a.m. and 4 p.m. so that they can be photographed. If you won't agree to that, it's no dice."

Villa, always a man who could be influenced by hard money, tugged at his black moustache. Suddenly he spat on the floor.

"I agree," he shouted. "No night attacks."

Thus began the only war in history coordinated to fit the whims of a movie script. Traveling aboard a special railroad car, the Hollywood crew became an integral part of Villa's army. And General Villa, the only field commander who ever had a film contract to worry about as well as the enemy, was equal to the challenge. Time and again his officers implored him: "Strike tonight!" But each time Villa replied: "No. This war we fight for the moving pictures."

Toward the end of January, 1914, Villa's troops had won everything along the border except the Federal stronghold at Ojinaga — the hamlet across the border from Presidio, Texas. Arriving at Ojinaga, Villa's officers wheeled their guns into position. But Villa refused to attack.

"We wait," he said. "The movie cameras are not yet in position."

When the train carrying the movie crew arrived two hours later, General Villa then gave the order to attack and Ojinaga fell.

On January 22, the first films of the war were shown in Mutual's New York projection room. Among those invited for the screening was Francisco Madero, Sr., father of Villa's special hero, the martyred president of Mexico. The Madero family had fled to New York for safety except for Raoul, the younger brother of the slain president. He was missing and presumed dead.

Shortly after the film began, however, the senior Madero suddenly jumped to his feet and shouted with excitement. There riding alongside Villa was Raoul, very much alive and, for the moment, safe.

Although Madero was delighted with the film, the Mutual executives were not. There were too many shots of Villa on his horse and not enough action shots of the war. Word was sent to L.M. Burrud, the ace cameraman that Mutual had sent to Mexico, to step up the realism.

Villa was cooperative. One morning he told the Mutual staff: "That shelling barrage you asked for — you'll get it today."

He took the camera crew to a nearby hill and pointed to a line of tents.

"A federal outpost," he explained.

As soon as the cameras were set, the order to fire was given. Field pieces smoked and shells blasted the enemy, surprised in their hillside encampment. Bodies hurtled skyward and tents were reduced to burning rubble.

The Mutual crew was delighted. These were the best and bloodiest shots of the war. Indeed, they should have been. Only later was it learned that the wily Villa had trained his devastating artillery on a defenseless prisoner of war camp.

These gory pictures were never shown in a theatre, however. In fact, the war that was waged for the cameras never reached the screen at all. When all of the footage was developed, there were still too many shots of Villa and not enough of the armies in action. The whole project was junked.

Villa, however, still wanted a movie and so did Mutual. In March, Aitken journeyed from New York to Juarez for a personal meeting with the revolutionary leader. He told him that there could never be a really good movie made without a script and a director. Villa agreed and signed a new contract.

This time, Mutual would do a film called *The Life of Pan-*

cho Villa. The war scenes would be shot on the studio lot in California and these would be interspersed with films of General Villa in action. To guarantee that it would be a real epic, no less a director than D. W. Griffith was selected to produce it.

Whether *The Life of Pancho Villa* would have made Griffith even more famous than he was, the world was never to know. After the film was finished, stockholders of Mutual got into an argument over the ownership of the negative. In the midst of their wrangling, it disappeared and never has been found.

A portion of some of the footage originally shot in the war that was deliberately staged for the cameras finally got before the public in the mid-1930s. A roadshow film called *Bring 'Em Back Dead* was a collection of newsreels about such infamous characters as John Dillinger, Clyde Barrow and Bonnie Parker and their likes. It included some of the pictures of Villa's shelling of his defenseless prisoners.

And what of Villa himself? He got to Mexico City and, for a few months, was in favor with President Emiliano Zapata, the rebel leader from the south. By 1915, however, Generals Obregon and Carranza, once his allies, had sent him back to oblivion in the mountains of Chihuahua.

He made one last attempt to be a *conquistador.* He began raiding towns in New Mexico, hoping he would anger the U. S. into a war with Mexico. President Wilson responded by sending General John J. Pershing and 12,000 troops to get the bandit "dead or alive." Villa escaped and lived peaceably on his beautiful hacienda in northern Mexico. In 1923, his car was ambushed and he died in a hail of assassins' bullets.

Ten years after his death, he finally got in the movies. But the Pancho Villa that appeared on the screen had Wallace Beery in the title role.

H.C. (Dutch) Dillingham, "anchor man" on the nation's first broadcast of a football game (The University of Texas vs. the Aggies) in 1919.
—Courtesy Texas A&M University

The Broadcast That Put
Football in the Living Room

On Thanksgiving Day, 1919, the Aggies of Texas A&M University hosted the Longhorns of The University of Texas in a football game at College Station that was destined for a niche in the history of sports.

It was not a game that provided much excitement for the 15,000 fans who sat in the chill of the old wooden stands. The Aggies, on their way to Coach Dana X. Bible's second Southwest Conference championship, took early control of the ball. Recovering a Longhorn fumble on the Texas 20, Roswell Higginbotham took the ball over for the last two yards at the beginning of the second quarter for the only score of the game. Except for one threat when Texas penetrated the A&M five-yard line, it was the Aggies all the way.

If action on the field was dull, it was anything but in the press box. There an event was going on which was destined to change football from a sport that required the active participation of players and fans to a new kind of living-room entertainment. From Kyle Field that day originated the world's first radio broadcast of a sports event.

Broadcasting the game was the brainchild of a couple of electrical engineering students named William A. (Dock) Tolson and H.C. Dillingham. Mastermind of the project was Tolson. He was interested in this new gimmick called radio and thought it might be fun to transmit a play-by-play account of the traditional game over the air. Neither he nor Dillingham, who was destined to do the actual broadcast, even had a transmitter when the idea was conceived. Putting one together was no easy task, either.

The only radio equipment available to the public in College Station at the time were pliers and copper wire that could be purchased at a local hardware store. To build even the smallest transmitter, Tolson and Dillingham borrowed whatever parts they could find from departments throughout the school.

"One vital part came from an electric fan which just accidentally fell from the window sill of this professor's office," Tolson wrote years later in an account of the broadcast preserved in the A&M archives. "The fan's blades were ruined in the two-story fall, but the motor worked fine."

Since the students had no microphone, there was no thought of a voice broadcast. But they did have a discarded telegraph key and they did know the old Continental code. They decided that they would describe the action on the field in dots and dashes, using a long set of initials for each movement of the ball.

Head Coach Bible helped them develop a special code of abbreviated terms which, when translated, would describe the play-by-play. "TB A 40Y" decoded into "Texas' ball on the Aggies' 40-yard line." And "T FP 3Y L" meant that Texas had tried a forward pass but lost three yards.

Once the equipment was ready and the code was worked out, the students wrote letters to newspapers around the state asking them if they'd be interested in receiving the broadcast. They wrote newspapers rather than offering the broadcast to the public for one good reason — almost nobody in 1919 had any home equipment for receiving coded radio transmissions. However, the newspapers (and the few existing radio stations) all wanted to receive the broadcast. The students kept a mimeograph machine working overtime getting copies of their abbreviated code in the mail to those who would have to translate it.

When Thanksgiving Day afternoon arrived, Dock Tolson was unable to take part in the broadcast. He had to take his regular place as trumpet player in the Aggie band. The assignment went to Dillingham, and it was he who tapped out to a waiting world the first broadcast of a sporting event ever transmitted in the world.

Thus began the transition of football from a game that required the fan to be present in the stadium to one that now requires only a good color television set, an easy chair and the appropriate refreshments. Not only was history made on that Texas Thanksgiving Day in 1919, but the lifestyle of a nation was changed, too.

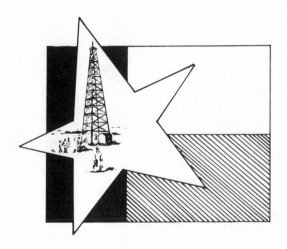

William Marsh Rice was an adopted Texan who dreamed of endowing a great university, but his secretary and an attorney had other plans for using his great fortune.

—Courtesy Rice University

Rice University:
The School a Murder Built

A suspicious bank clerk and smart police work combined to give Houston its great Rice University — one of the top-ranking colleges in the United States today.

The university owes its existence to a $10 million endowment left to it in 1910 by an elderly man who did not forget that he arrived in Texas penniless and left with a fortune. Had it not been for a macabre series of events, however, Rice University might have been located in New Jersey instead of Houston. And it might never have existed at all if a New York bank clerk hadn't refused to cash a check.

Rice University's unique story really begins on a crisp, fall morning in 1839. William Marsh Rice, age twenty-two and carrying only ninety pounds on his five foot three frame, stepped off the packet *Bayou City* when it docked at the foot of Houston's Main Street. Rice, a school dropout from Springfield, Massachusetts, had come to Texas to seek his fortune.

Before leaving Springfield, Rice had clerked in a country store from the age of fourteen. At twenty-one, he bought the establishment, but decided a year later to take his merchandise to Texas and make a new start. He sent his inventory to Galveston aboard a ship while he traveled overland and by inland waterways. It was lucky that he did because the ship carrying his goods sank before reaching Galveston.

Although Rice arrived in Houston broke, he didn't stay that way long. He walked into the old Ben Milam Hotel and made the manager a proposition: He volunteered to furnish

89

and serve the liquors in the hotel bar in exchange for room and board and three dollars a day. From this beginning as a bartender, Rice began building a business empire — in cotton, importing and exporting, wholesale groceries, shipping and railroads.

Despite the great wealth he finally amassed, Rice remained what one of his biographers described "as a rather colorless personality to whom colorful things happened with regularity." Uneducated, Rice never bothered to improve his knowledge and limited his reading to newspapers. He disliked music, had no feel for art and little interest in the social amenities pursued by so many of the rich.

After the Civil War, his fortune made and secure, Rice and his second wife (the first had died in 1863) moved to New York. He also owned a farm in New Jersey, and the couple shuttled between the farm, their Manhattan home and Houston for years.

Meanwhile, Rice conceived the idea of willing his fortune to found an educational institution for "poor male fatherless orphan children" of Texas and New Jersey. He specified that it be located on his New Jersey estate. Later he changed his mind and chose Houston as the site because: "Texas received me when I was penniless, without friends or even acquaintances, and now in the evening of my life, I recognize my obligation to her and to her children."

Rice made an initial gift of $200,000 for such an institute, but he had reckoned without his wife. When she died in 1896, she used Texas's community property laws as the basis for her will and she left her half of Rice's estate to a number of philanthropies. Rice, who wanted his entire fortune to go to the university of his dreams, went to court to break his wife's will. He sought to prove that, as a legal resident of New York, the community property laws of Texas did not apply.

One of the attorneys opposing him in court was Albert T. Patrick, a graduate of Texas A&M University. One of his great and good friends was one Charles F. Jones, secretary and general factotum to Mr. Rice. When the courts ruled in favor of Rice and kept the fortune intact, the attorney and the secretary decided that there were other ways to keep the Rice millions from being used to build a university.

Their plan called for Patrick to rewrite Rice's will. The proposed grant for an educational institute was deleted and

Patrick was made the residual heir. Rice, then eighty, couldn't live much longer so Patrick and Jones sat back to wait for the millionaire to die. When Rice's health refused to falter, they decided to help along his demise with mercury pills which Patrick obtained and Jones slipped into his food.

The mercury was slowly undermining the old man's health and Patrick and Jones saw no reason to hasten matters. Then the attorney learned that Rice was shipping off $250,000 to Houston to rebuild a cottonseed mill that had been destroyed by fire and the pair decided they would rather keep this quarter of a million as a part of their eventual loot. On September 23, 1900, as Rice slept, Jones slipped into his bedroom and held a sponge soaked with chloroform to his employer's face until he was dead.

It is likely that Mr. Rice's death would have gone into the records as resulting from the infirmities of age if Patrick and Jones had been willing to wait even a few days before getting their hands on some of the money. Instead they immediately dispatched a young man named David L. Short to the banking house of S.M. Swenson and Sons to cash a couple of checks. The certified checks, one for $25,000 and one for $65,000, were signed by William M. Rice, who was well known at the bank, and were made out to one "Abbert L. Patrick." Short said that Patrick was Rice's attorney.

John W. Wallace, the teller to whom the checks were presented for payment, had a sharp eye. He noted that while the checks were made out to "Abbert L. Patrick" they were endorsed "Albert L. Patrick" and he rejected them. Short explained that this was a typographical error which Mr. Rice would happily correct. He returned a short time later with the two checks properly made out and properly endorsed. Wallace, however, was still suspicious and asked a co-worker, Walter O. Weatherbee, to compare the signature of Mr. Rice with other cancelled checks in the bank's file.

Weatherbee decided that there was some irregularity about the signature and called Mr. Rice at his Hotel Berkshire apartment to verify the authenticity of the checks. Jones, the secretary, answered. He said that Mr. Rice had gone out. Jones assured Weatherbee, however, that he had personally made out the checks for Mr. Rice's signature and apologized for misspelling Patrick's first name.

Neither Wallace nor Weatherbee were satisfied and asked the bank's head, Swen Swenson, to telephone. When Jones again answered the call, Swenson insisted on talking with Rice.

"That is impossible," Jones replied. "Mr. Rice is dead." He did not elaborate.

Now thoroughly mystified, Swenson not only refused to honor the checks, but called the District Attorney. The latter immediately ordered detectives to interview both Jones, the secretary, and Patrick, the attorney. He also asked for an autopsy.

Patrick was smilingly cooperative. He said that the two checks, plus two others for $135,000 and $25,000 which another bank had cashed without question, constituted a trust fund for a compromise settlement of $1,500,000 in lawsuits which had plagued the financier. He also pointed out that an autopsy wasn't needed since Rice's personal physician had signed the death certificate giving "heart failure and old age" as the causes of death.

As the investigation continued, James A. Baker of Houston, Rice's Texas attorney and one of the executors of the will Rice had made in 1896, arrived. He brought the will with him. It left some small bequests to a number of Rice's relatives, but the $10 million bulk was to found an institution "for the advancement of literature, science and art."

The day Baker filed the will for probate, Patrick produced his. It was dated June 30, 1900. It left $75,000 to each relative, $250,000 to found a school in Houston and the rest to Patrick.

A few days later, the autopsy surgeon reported that he had found mercury in Rice's stomach and more in his intestines. He said that indications were that the poison "had been introduced into the body of the deceased probably several hours, possibly several days previous to his death."

Police now were sure that they were on the trail of a shrewd embezzler who had tried to design a perfect murder to hide his theft. Proving this theory wasn't that simple, however.

A break came shortly after when Patrick was ordered by the court to file the will in his possession for probate. It was the first opportunity that police handwriting experts had had to examine it. They discovered that the signature of Rice was identical with that on the checks — a tracing. Who the forger was remained a mystery.

Then, on April 2, 1901, almost seven months after Rice's death, the financier's young secretary-valet told police the bizarre story. Patrick had never been Rice's attorney. The two had met casually during the proceedings to break Mrs. Rice's will and conceived the bizarre scheme that would make millionaires of both men when the financier died.

Jones admitted that he had typed up the false will at Patrick's direction, had prepared the bogus checks and traced Rice's signature, had administered the mercury tablets and had, indeed, murdered his boss with chloroform when the old man refused to die. Police arrested both and charged them with murder.

Because he had turned state's evidence, Jones was given immunity even though he was the confessed murderer. Patrick was sentenced to death, but this was commuted to life imprisonment and later he was given a full pardon. Jones remained in Texas, became wealthy in his own right and lived until 1954 when he shot himself at the age of 83 in his Baytown home. Patrick moved to Tulsa, Oklahoma, after his release from prison, also became well-to-do and died in 1940 at the age of 74.

The confessions of Jones and the conviction of Patrick, however, did not end the wrangle over the Rice estate. The fight over the validity of Mrs. Rice's will continued. Some of her legatees received settlements and others lost in court fights. It was seven years after Rice's murder that the trustees of the proposed institute finally received what was left of the estate: about $8 million. And five years later, on September 23, 1912, the first students went to class on the campus of the school which the once penniless Yankee had dreamed about for the state where he had found opportunity.

Rice University exists, however, not only because of the endowment William Marsh Rice provided it. It also owes its heritage to a young bank clerk without whose suspicions a fortune would have been embezzled and two murderers never punished. Thus Rice is the only educational institution in the world that owes its life to an alert banker and good police work.

Jacob Brodbeck was a Fredericksburg schoolmaster who built and flew an airplane thirty-eight years before the Wright brothers.
—Photo courtesy of E.E. Brodbeck from U.T. Institute of Texan Cultures

Was a Texan
The First Man to Fly?

History to the contrary, there is growing evidence that Orville and Wilbur Wright were not the first human beings to build and fly an airplane under its own power.

At least three Texans apparently beat the Wrights into the skies. Two of them produced eyewitnesses to prove their claim. The third built an airship and sold stock in a projected airline (see Chapter 3, "The Airship Inspired by the *Bible*"), but there is no record that his machine ever got off the ground.

One, W.D. Custead, a railroad telegrapher in McLennan County, was ostensibly flitting about the Central Texas blue skies a half dozen years before the Wrights were airborne. However, neither Custead, the telegrapher, not Burrell, the preacher-inventor, can contest the record of Jacob Brodbeck for the niche history presently accords the brothers Wright. Brodbeck built and flew his airplane in Texas in 1865, before Orville and Wilbur Wright were born.

Brodbeck was born in 1821 in Württemberg, Germany, was educated as a teacher and was a schoolmaster for six years in his home town. Except that it provided a livelihood, teaching held little interest for him. He was fascinated by the source of energy and the power it produced and his special interest was the coiled spring. He spent much of his spare time trying to build a spring-powered clock that would run without winding; he wanted to present it to the Kaiser as a gift.

When he was twenty-five, Brodbeck decided to join the German immigration to Texas. He settled at Fredericksburg, in the Hill Country, and became the second schoolmaster at the *Vereins Kirche*, the town's octagonal church that also doubled as a classroom. He also taught in other nearby German communities, worked for awhile as county surveyor and played the organ in area churches. He spent every spare moment, however, inventing toys — especially those which could be powered by a coiled spring.

They really weren't toys by today's standards; rather they were models of the ideas that poured from Brodbeck's inventive mind. His special love was a miniature airplane that would fly under its own power when its coiled spring was wound. And he was certain that if the toy would fly, he could also build a plane with a larger spring that would carry a man into the air.

Brodbeck had learned the principles of aerodynamics by watching the birds. He observed that they flew on the same principle as the united working of the kite and the parachute. Thus be believed that if he could build a plane that would conform to these principles of aerodynamics, it should be able to carry a human being. He set about to prove it.

As with many inventors, however, Brodbeck found it difficult to find the money for his idea. Seven years after arriving in Texas, he had married an attractive *fraulein* named Marie Christina Behrens. Several of what was to become a family of twelve children already had arrived and Brodbeck's meager salary as a school teacher was barely enough to keep them. He decided to move to San Antonio in an effort to improve his finances.

The Brodbecks didn't find the going much easier in the Alamo City. He did become inspector of schools at a salary considerably above that of a teacher, but he also had to make wine on the side to supplement his income. He made the product at his modest home, fermenting it in twenty-gallon barrels. Customers apparently liked it, however, because local saloons bought all that he could produce.

With profits from the wine business, Brodbeck began work on a full size model of his plane. As word got around among fellow Germans in the community that one of their number was working on a machine in which a man could fly, several offered to help finance the project. They bought shares at $1.25 each, with Brodbeck promising to repay the cost of the stock plus a share of the profits if his airplane flew and went into commercial production.

Brodbeck was confident that his plane would fly. It would, of course, be powered by a coiled spring — the energy source he loved best. Actually he had no other choice. Even the smallest steam engine available in 1864 was so heavy that it could never lift its own weight, plus a vehicle and that of a "driver." The internal combustion engine had not been invented. Thus the coiled spring was the only available power.

By early 1865, Brodbeck had completed his model. It had two partly movable wings, a rudder for steering and a screw propeller. And it was powered by a huge coil spring — one that had to be rewound constantly by the pilot while the uncoiling of the other end provided the energy to turn the propeller.

There were no newspaper reporters on hand the day Brodbeck decided to try his wings over the mesquite covered hills west of San Antonio. Even he failed to record the date of the experiment, except that it was in the early spring. However, there were a number of witnesses to the flight and one of them wrote a brief account of it. The witness attested to the fact that the craft did take off and that it reached treetop level. But the coiled spring which had worked so perfectly in the toy models Brodbeck had made didn't perform as expected. The tension went down rapidly — and so did the airplane. Brodbeck wasn't injured, but the plane was a total loss.

Brodbeck refused to be discouraged. He decided to try to build a steam engine small enough and light enough to power the plane. His investors, however, refused any more support. Having watched their investment crumple after less than sixty seconds of flight, they decided to keep their cash in their pockets.

With his own capital also in the wreckage of the plane, Brodbeck hoped to attract a new set of investors. He advertised in Texas newspapers asking readers to back his idea with their dollars. They didn't respond. Brodbeck then took to the lecture circuit hoping that he could raise money by outlining in person his plans to build a machine that would enable man to fly like a bird. The sky, he said, was the new frontier.

"To take advantage of my aeroplane one must have a steam engine that weighs no more than 40,000 to 45,000 pounds," he told his audiences. "With the increased weight of 40,000 pounds a steam engine of eighty horsepower should be made out of cast iron and will produce an aeroplane that should give an acceleration of 100 miles per hour on a quiet atmosphere."

Audiences came to listen to the German schoolmaster who believed that he could provide a vehicle in which man could fly, but they didn't respond with money. Most of his listeners simply didn't believe that what he proposed was possible; almost none of them understood the long explanations of the theories of aerodynamics with which he tried to enlighten them. In an era when the railroad was still a novelty to most of the nation, the people couldn't comprehend Brodbeck's predictions on the salutary effects that air transport would someday have on the economy of the world.

His final plea was short, dramatic and called for immediate action: "Should not every man, because of the importance of the object, give everything in his power to help me complete my experiment? Capitalists and business should be interested enough to offer their aid in its completion."

They were not, and Brodbeck became increasingly discouraged. Then one night after a lecture in a Michigan town, somebody stole the drawings of his proposed aeroplane and most of his research notes. He had not taken the precaution to make copies of either, and so, much of his life work was lost to a thief.

Virtually bankrupt and embittered at his inability to attract new investors, Brodbeck returned to Texas. He settled on a small farm near Luckenbach, a few miles from Fredericksburg. There he would live out his life, his dream of giving wings to man unrealized.

The plans and notes stolen from him were never found. But when Orville and Wilbur Wright put their motor-powered plane into the air at Kitty Hawk more than three decades later, some of those who had seen Brodbeck's plane were amazed at the resemblance in the design of his airplane and that of the Wright brothers. Was it possible that Jacob Brodbeck's plans had, somehow, been the basis for the design the Wright brothers used?

If the old inventor had any such ideas, he kept them to himself. Seven years later, at age ninety, he died. He had proved conclusively that man could fly, and he might be remembered today by history as the father of aviation except for one thing. He had believed that the coil spring which powered his airplane could be rewound by the pilot as it unwound. It couldn't.

Santa Anna and
the Legacy of Chewing Gum

General Antonio Lopez de Santa Anna is remembered by history as a womanizer, a successful con man and the leader of the army that slaughtered the defenders of the Alamo. The historians, however, usually overlook the fact that he also was responsible for introducing modern chewing gum to the world.

Santa Anna actually was a Johnny-come-lately to that mass of humanity addicted to chewing. The ancient Greeks chomped on a variety of native waxes. Cleopatra often gave Mark Anthony flavored resin to chew and thus improve his halitosis as they trysted aboard her barge on the Nile. Long before the first Spanish conquistador arrived in what now is Mexico, the pre-Columbian Indians had discovered that the wax from the cypress, cedar and sweet gum trees made an acceptable chew.

It remained for Santa Anna, however, to recognize both the military and financial possibilities of mastication. When he and his invading Mexican Army were cutting a wide swath through Texas in the early months of 1836, the general found that having something to munch on helped to keep his soldiers relaxed. He kept them supplied with chicle, the wax of the sapodilla tree.

Perhaps the troops were contentedly chewing their cuds of chicle on April 21, 1836, at San Jacinto. If they were, that's a footnote that has been lost to history. They were reported to have been enjoying *siesta* while their general dallied with a beautiful mulatto girl in his tent. At any rate, General Sam

Because General Santa Anna encouraged his Mexican Army to chew chicle to relieve tension, he deserves some of the credit for inventing the chewing gum of today.

— Photo from *Harper's Weekly*, 1867,
in U.T. Institute of Texan Cultures Collection

Houston and his Texian Army attacked and eighteen minutes later, the battle was over and Santa Anna was a prisoner.

When a war ends, there always is much clean-up work to be done by the diplomats and Houston kept Santa Anna as his unwilling guest for almost a year. Military etiquette being what it is, the Texas commander-in-chief spared his Mexican counterpart as many discomforts and humiliations as possible. It happened that the Texian Army had captured Santa Anna's bed (but not his bedmate) when they took the general and Houston allowed him to sleep on his personal couch the first night after the battle. The Texians, lacking such comforts, slept on the ground.

For the ten months it required to hammer out the treaty with Mexico, Santa Anna and his staff were shunted about as if they were on a conducted tour. From San Jacinto they were moved to Velasco and then to Quintana. Next they were held at Columbia and then moved to the Phelps plantation at Orozimba. During this period, Santa Anna had little to do but munch on his chicle and make friends with some of his captors. One of these was named Gilbert L. Thompson.

In February, 1837, Thompson was back in his native New York and Santa Anna finally was allowed to return to Mexico. By 1839, he had been reelected president of the country again — an office he was to be in and out of several times before his constituents finally threw him out and forced him into hiding. Santa Anna hurriedly sent a message to New York asking his friend, Thompson, for help.

Over the years, Thompson had acquired wealth and his friendship with the former dictator had strengthened. When the SOS came, Thompson dispatched his yacht to Mexico and smuggled Santa Anna out of the country. The general managed to make his escape with a wardrobe of military uniforms, his jeweled walking stick and his inevitable supply of chicle. He also took along his secretary, Rudolph Napegy.

Apparently Santa Anna also took along considerable gold when he made his exit. Not long after he arrived in New York, his lavish spending, his ornate uniforms and his conversational wit endeared him to Staten Island society. He bought a mansion, staffed it well and entertained often. His business affairs were left almost entirely to the capable hands of Napegy.

Business kept Napegy traveling frequently from Staten Is-

land over to Manhattan and he was a regular passenger on the
ferry between the two. The ferry docked at the foot of Liberty
Street, a block away from the Cortlandt Street shop of one
Thomas Adams, a dealer in glass and a sometime inventor. Napegy usually stopped at Adams's shop on his walk uptown and
admired the window displays. These stops led to inquiries
about the purchase of certain items and, in time, to social visits
with Adams.

Talk got around one day to Adams's interest in inventions
and he told Napegy that he was trying to find a way to adulterate rubber. The secretary, remembering the chicle his boss had
brought along, thought it might be helpful in the adulteration
process. The next time he was in Manhattan, he brought
Adams a supply. The inventor put some chemists to work ex-
perimenting with the stuff but the results were negative and
he gave up on the idea.

Meanwhile on Staten Island, "Santy" — as his new American friends were wont to call him — had his own project in
work. At the proper time, he planned to sell what he would call
"first mortgage bonds" supposedly secured by his "palaces and
grounds" in Mexico and paying a high interest rate. That he no
longer had any kind of habitation in Mexico that he could call
his own worried Santa Anna not a whit. He knew that his rich
New York intimates would fall for the scheme and he could return home with his pockets lined with U. S. gold.

Santa Anna probably knew nothing of the experiments
with his chicle that Napegy had initiated with Adams and the
entire incident might have been forgotten except for chance.
Not long after he had given up his efforts to adulterate rubber,
Adams stopped in a Jersey City drugstore one day to pick up a
prescription. While waiting, a young lady walked in and asked
for a package of paraffin chewing gum.

"Is there much sale for paraffin gum?" Adams asked the
druggist.

"Not really," was the reply. "Too hard to chew."

Suddenly Adams remembered something. During the unsuccessful rubber experiment, the chemists often would break
off a piece of the chicle and chew it. They seemed to enjoy
chomping on it as they worked and this gave Adams an idea.

At home that evening, he and his son, Horatio, took some
chicle, put it in a pan of hot water and left it there until it had

the consistency of putty. Then he rolled the stuff into little balls and let it cool. A couple of days later, Adams dropped off a supply at the Jersey City drugstore, asked the druggist to let his customers try it. Thus the chewing gum boom was born.

From the beginning, Adams's product was a good and steady seller. He realized, however, that kneading the chicle into balls was too time-consuming and expensive. He invented a machine that ran the product into long, thin strips. The seller then would cut off the strips into lengths that he could sell for a penny.

On February 14, 1871, Adams patented his new chewing gum. By this time he had improved it by adding flavorings and the Adams Gum Company became preeminent in its field. Soon brand names like its Chiclets and Dentyne would become household words all around the world.

Apparently neither Napegy nor his boss, Santa Anna, profited from the chewing gum bonanza, however. Four years before Adams launched his company, Santa Anna had managed to sell $750,000 worth of his bonds to unwary Americans and had returned to Mexico. Shortly after he landed in Vera Cruz in 1867, he was arrested by Mexican authorities. A few months later, he was exiled again and sought a haven in Cuba and later in Nassau. The fate of his secretary has been lost to history.

It would have been to the financial benefit of both Santa Anna and Napegy if they had joined forces with Adams. As the nineteenth century wore on, dozens of new companies entered the chewing gum field and the competition became fierce. By 1899 there were so many manufacturers turning out the product that they decided to form a protective trust. The Adams Company, as leaders in the field, helped organize the new operation which came to be known as the American Chicle Company. It dominated the world market until the early 1900s when William Wrigley, Jr., a door-to-door salesman of household products, became the new success with a brand of chewing gum called "Spearmint."

While others were making millions out of his chicle, Santa Anna was spending the dollars he had conned out of his New York pals with his worthless bonds. In 1874, when a forgiving Mexican government finally allowed the old dictator back in his homeland, he arrived penniless and ill. The money he had obtained from his bond sales was never repaid, yet there is no record that any of the purchasers of the paper ever pressed a claim. Today the bonds, each signed personally by Antonio Lopez de Santa Anna, are prized by collectors. One is on display at The University of Texas Institute of Texan Cultures in San Antonio.

Blind, destitute, and almost forgotten by the country he had served numerous times as president and dictator, Santa Anna died June 21, 1876. The only notice of his death appeared as a paragraph in *Two Republics*, a leading Mexican newspaper of the times. The account said

> General Antonio Lopez de Santa Anna died in this city on the 21st inst. However he may have been condemned by parties, his career formed a brilliant and important part of the history of Mexico, and future historians will differ in their judgment of his merits. Santa Anna outlived his usefulness and his ambitions. He died at the ripe old age of 84. Peace to his ashes.

There was no mention that his greatest legacy to the world may have been chewing gum.

The Civil War?
It Ended in Texas!

Historians usually fail to mention it, and Yankees don't believe it, but the fact is that the last battle of the Civil War was fought in Texas. It happened on May 13, 1865, exactly thirty-four days after the war supposedly had come to an end.

Why a battle was fought a month after General Robert E. Lee surrendered the Confederacy to General U. S. Grant's Union forces at Appomattox Court House, Virginia, on April 9, 1865, remains one of the mysteries of history. Was it true, as some historians argue, that neither side knew that the conflict between the States had ended? Or was it because General Grant, later to become president of the united States, didn't want the war to end until Archduke Ferdinand Maximilian had been unseated as emperor of Mexico?

The installation of Maximilian as ruler of Mexico would, Grant felt, be an impediment to the United States once the war ended. France and Austria, sympathetic to the cause of the Confederacy, had taken advantage of the Civil War to ignore the Monroe Doctrine and install Maximilian as Mexico's ruler. Mexican rebels, resentful of being ruled by an Austrian, organized guerilla bands to oppose Maximilian. And since their emperor, at the insistence of France and Austria, supported the South, they took the side of the Union in the conflict. As a result, fighting between Mexican government troops and those of the rebels frequently spilled across the Rio Grande into Texas.

Colonel John S. (Rip) Ford who, since 1861, had been in the Rio Grande Valley recruiting and commanding a volunteer

Colonel John S. (Rip) Ford was in command when the last battle of the Civil War was fought in the Rio Grande Valley thirty-four days after Lee surrendered the Confederacy.

— Photo courtesy Ford de Cordova,
U.T. Institute of Texan Cultures Collection

force to keep the area under control of the South, naturally co-operated with Maximilian's forces. Thus he had succeeded in keeping Brownsville an open port, operating through Bagdad on the Mexican side of the river. Although Federal forces had taken Brazos Island, near the mouth of the Rio Grande, and other Union troops had blockaded or captured almost every other southern port, Ford had managed to keep control of both Fort Brown and the port of Brownsville.

Thousands of bales of cotton were stored at Brownsville for shipment to Mexico through Bagdad. They were to be ex-changed with Emperor Maximilian for munitions and food and clothing — items the South sorely needed. General Grant, on the other hand, wanted to capture the cotton before it went to Mexico and probably ordered his troops to attack despite the fact that the war had ended officially.

There is considerable logic in the historical record to sup-port this thesis. Throughout the spring of 1865, the Union and Confederate troops in the Rio Grande Valley had lived in peaceful coexistence. Except for occasional forays by the Union troops from Brazos Island, there had been no fighting for many weeks. And it is almost certain that between April 9, when Lee surrendered to Grant, and May 13, word reached the Union troops that the war was over.

However, on May 11, 1865, 250 men of the 62nd U.S. Col-ored Infantry and 52 men of the Second Texas (Union) Cavalry were ordered by Lieutenant Colonel T.H. Barrett to proceed from Brazos Island in a blinding rainstorm. Captain James Hancock commanded this advance force and they managed to cross Boca Chica and get to the mainland. At 8:30 a.m. the next day, they met a Confederate battalion commanded by Captain W.N. Robinson at Palmetto (sometimes called Palmito Ranch). There was some skirmishing before the Confederates retreated into the brush, leaving a number of horses, cattle and supplies to the Federals.

The Yankees set fire to the ranch and retired to another where they camped for the night. By the next morning, Colonel Barrett arrived with some 200 reinforcements and for the next twelve hours, the two forces skirmished in and around Pal-metto. Meanwhile word had reached Colonel Ford at Browns-ville of the Union force's "invasion" and he gathered all of his available troops and moved east with six field guns toward the battlefront.

By 3 p.m. on May 13, Ford's column had joined Captain Robinson and found the troops still skirmishing. Colonel Ford took immediate command and ordered an attack on the left flank of the Federals. At the first volley from the Confederates, the black troops stampeded in retreat. They soon regrouped, however, to plan a second try at overrunning the Confederates.

Rip Ford, whose career had included fighting Indians, was confident that he could counterattack and defeat the Union troops despite the fact that he was outnumbered. He rode up and down the line shouting: "Men, we have whipped the enemy in all of our previous fights! We can do it again!"

The troops responded with cheers and he raised his six-shooter and ordered a charge. From that point on, it became a rout instead of a battle. The Confederates rushed forward, shooting at everything that moved. Once again, the men of Morton's Rifles — a crack regiment of black troops — broke ranks and fled. Within a few minutes, the light artillery of the Confederates had broken the entire Federal line.

Colonel Ford ordered hot pursuit. The Federals, however, headed toward a levee across the *resaca* — a shortcut to their camp on Brazos Island. Although the Confederates made a concentrated attack on the levee, most of the enemy made it across, reformed and made another stand. By the time both forces got into fighting position, however, the sun had gone down and both sides elected to retire for the night.

Once the Federals got back to the safety of Brazos Island, there was little reason for the Confederates to continue the battle anyway. Fewer than 300 Federals had been ordered into the fight and another 1,400 had remained on the island. Any effort on the part of the Confederates to take their position probably would have been disastrous.

Brigadier General J.E. Slaughter, who had been placed in command of the Confederates earlier over the protests of Colonel Ford, was away from headquarters when the Union attack began. When he did arrive at the action later with another battalion to reinforce Ford's troops, his first order was to charge the Yankees anyway. Ford refused.

There had been bad blood between the two from the time

General Slaughter had been named commander of the Western Sub-District. Ford, who for four years had managed to keep the Rio Grande Valley under Confederate control and trade with Mexico open, resented having a senior officer imposed on his command. He felt, probably with justification, that he should have been promoted to brigadier and allowed to see the war to its conclusion. He also was aware that Slaughter was anything but popular with the soldiers and Ford believed that a field commander who wasn't respected by his men could not lead in battle.

At any rate, the two feuded constantly and their personal argument continued on the night of May 13 as the Confederates set up camp near the Palmetto Ranch. In refusing to attack the retreating Union Forces, Ford had blatantly disobeyed the order of his commanding officer and Slaughter wanted his hide. But Ford, never one to capitulate when he believed he was in the right, told the general bluntly that his order was stupid. He pointed out that any good field commander would never have issued such an order when it was apparent that his men were already so battle-weary that they could barely shoulder their rifles.

As darkness settled, their argument degenerated into a feud over where they would camp. Slaughter liked the idea of remaining near Brazos Island; Ford insisted that this was too close to the enemy for comfort. The general argued that the Confederates owed it to the considerable number of Yankee prisoners they had taken to stop and let them have rest and food. Again Ford disobeyed his commander and ordered his troops to march on to a point eight miles north.

Such flagrant insubordination was more than Slaughter could take. He mounted his horse, took his personal staff and returned to Brownsville. Colonel Ford, delighted to be rid of his obnoxious boss, led his men and their prisoners to the safer campsite he had chosen.

It was there, as the troops were settling down for the night, that the War Between the States was to come to an end. A Federal gunboat, the S.S. *Isabella*, had entered the Rio Grande and anchored. Whether by accident or design, the ship lobbed a shell onto the mainland that landed about half way between the Union and Confederate camps. It did no damage, but it angered a seventeen-year-old private clad in gray. He leaped to his feet, grabbed his Enfield rifle and fired in the general direction of the gunboat.

His act made history because it was the last shot fired in the war. The next morning, the Union forces continued their withdrawal and Colonel Ford and his Confederates started back toward Brownsville. From their Union prisoners, they had learned that the South had fallen and that the long conflict that split a nation was over.

That night in Matamoros, across the river from Brownsville, they held a dinner, not in celebration of victory, but of Thanksgiving that the fighting was over. As special guests they invited the Union officers they had captured. It was a gesture of friendship to indicate that a great nation, so long devastated by internal strife, was united again.

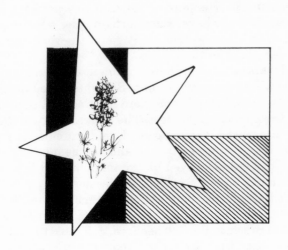

When Texas Sent
Mail by Missile

It probably wouldn't have happened except for sixteen-year-old Keith Rumbel's fascination with chemicals and his theory that a projectile could be the most innovative improvement in the postal service since the Pony Express.

So it came to pass that Keith's talents, plus the need of a Texas American Legion Post to raise money, resulted in the first and only effort in history to transport mail between two countries by rocket. It happened on July 2, 1936, and the incident has been all but forgotten except among stamp collectors and visitors to the McAllen Museum in the Rio Grande Valley.

As a student in McAllen High School, young Rumbel had developed an early interest in explosives and also in printing. Propellants held a special fascination for him and he had built and successfully fired several small rockets from his backyard. When he wasn't busy with his chemicals, he usually was at work on a small printing press his father, O.K. Rumbel, had given him as a present.

The elder Rumbel also happened to be the historian of Loyal Service Post Number 37 of the American Legion. Not long before, Mr. Rumbel's Legion Post had decided to do what no other group of Legionnaires in the southwest had ever attempted before and that was to finance and build their own headquarters. By early in 1936, the building was completed but the debt on it had not been paid. The veterans of World War

I were looking around for a way to pay off the mortgage before their planned dedication of the headquarters on July 2.

At dinner one evening, father and son were discussing the Legion's problem when Keith suggested a solution. Why not experiment with sending mail by rocket between the United States and Mexico?

The idea wasn't as farfetched as it may have seemed at the time. As early as 1928, rockets had been used to transport mail in some experiments in Europe. At least three such efforts had also been tried in the United States with some success. Nobody, however, had attempted to send rocket mail between two countries and Keith believed that such an experiment, coupled with his talents at the printing press, could put needed money in the coffers of Loyal Service Post Number 37.

The elder Rumbel, with every confidence in Keith's ability to produce both the necessary rockets and the supporting software, presented the idea to his fellow Legionnaires. They were enthusiastic and authorized Keith to go to work.

American and Mexican officialdom provided the first barrier to the project. Customs officers didn't like the idea of mail arriving and departing without their having scrutinized it first. Postal authorities balked at the idea of any kind of mail which didn't bear official postage stamps — and Keith Rumbel's plan called for the messages to carry stamps he would design and print.

Eventually, however, the bureaucratic hurdles were overcome by compromise. Keith could design and print some special triangular colored "rocket mail stamps" and these could be affixed to the "first day covers" he hoped collectors would buy. In addition, the two governments insisted that their own airmail stamps also would have to go on the mail. The U. S. cover would carry a sixteen-cent special delivery and the Mexican cover would carry that country's new forty-centavo version of *aereo corro*.

To raise funds for the Legion, Keith's special "rocket stamps" were offered at fifty cents each or two dollars for a bloc of four. Collectors who preferred to buy a "first day cover" that actually had been transported from one country to the other by rocket had to ante up one dollar. A total of 3,000 covers were to be printed and young Rumbel was convinced that each would one day become a valuable addition to any philatelist's collection.

Once approval of the project had been obtained from both countries, Keith began work on his rockets. Each was seven feet long and twelve inches in diameter. To make them as lightweight as possible (and to lessen the danger of maiming in case of premature explosion), he used laminated cardboard and fiberboard to form the bodies. A compartment in the nose and one just behind the center of the missile would carry the mail. The propellant was to be slow-burning and the trajectory was figured at about 1,000 feet.

The afternoon of July 2, 1936, was destined to be a memorable one in McAllen if not in the history of transport. Members of the Legion post, together with officials from both the United States and Mexico, gathered near the International Bridge at Hidalgo on the American side. Garland Adair of Austin, the Legion's state historian and ranking member of the organization present for the occasion, was given the honor of firing the first rocket.

Adair stepped up to the slipway, lit the missile and stepped back. There was a loud explosion as the rocket sped off, traveled about one hundred feet and then exploded, dumping its cargo of precious covers into the rain-swollen Rio Grande. A fragment struck a U.S. customs official but, because of the rocket's cardboard construction, the only damage was to his shirtfront.

For a few moments it appeared that the great rocket mail experiment was a failure. Then McAllen Mayor A.L. Landry stepped up and fired off the second. This one not only zoomed skyward but sailed high over the heads of the waiting officials on the Mexican side of the river. Instead of traveling 1,000 feet, as Keith had designed it to do, it roared into downtown Reynosa, skimmed past a parked car and slammed into the side of the town's favorite watering place, the U. S. Bar. Customers, uncertain as to whether they were being attacked by *bandidos* or if a new revolution had started, left their tequilas and beers and poured into the street.

Mexican customs officers were furious and promptly confiscated all that remained of the rocket and the contents of its undamaged mail compartments. Even they rated the rocket's trip a success, however, because of the great distance that it had traveled. Except for a few wrinkles that resulted from the landing, the mail was intact.

Elated with the success of Rocket Number 2, three others (some newspaper accounts at that time report that there was a fourth) were fired in order to get all of the covers to their destination. Then the official party crossed over into Mexico and repeated the process. Each of the rockets fired from Mexico landed safely in the United States, although the distance they traveled varied from 1,000 feet to almost one mile.

When it was all over, collectors had a total of 1,072 covers which had made the trip from McAllen to Mexico and 922 which had made the trip in reverse. Of those which had been dumped in the Rio Grande by Rocket Number 1, fifty-one eventually were recovered in various states of damage. The Mexican government held onto the 150 they confiscated in the incident at the U. S. Bar.

These 150 pieces of rocket mail were destined to write an unusual postscript to the experiment. Several months later, Bolton Hyde, commander of the McAllen Legion Post, convinced Mexican customs that they should release the covers they had confiscated. He gave them to Keith Rumbel's father who put them in a safety deposit box and then forgot about them.

In 1956, a McAllen bank officer discovered a safety deposit box which had been issued to the American Legion in 1936 and on which no rent had been paid in years. When the box was opened, there were the old covers. So Legion Post number 37 decided to hold another fund-raising event.

This time, however, the price of the rocket mail went up. Philatelists around the country were offered the remaining 150 covers at $5 each, one to a customer on a first come, first served basis. Orders poured into McAllen from throughout the world. Even the Smithsonian Institution in Washington and the Swiss Postal Museum were among the customers. And hundreds more wanted the scarce covers but couldn't get them.

Today one of the triangular stamps which Keith Rumbel designed and printed on his home press brings as much as $20 when collectors gather. One of the rocket mail experiment's "first day covers" with the proper postal cancellations has brought as much as $200. Visitors to the McAllen Museum, where a complete set of the stamps and covers are displayed along with photographs of the rocket shoot, are always trying to buy the exhibit.

The U.S. Postal Service, which was recalcitrant in permitting the attempt at rocket mail transport, apparently wasn't impressed by the experiment. Today it sometimes takes two days for mail to travel from McAllen to Reynosa although the post offices are a bare ten miles apart. The distance could be covered in ten seconds by one of Keith Rumbel's rockets, as he proved conclusively that day in 1936.

Old Rip: The Horned Toad
That Astounded the World

For more than half a century, one of Texas's most unique tourist attractions has been the embalmed body of a horned toad.

His name was "Old Rip" and he has rested in a glass casket in the lobby of the Eastland County Courthouse since he froze to death January 19, 1929. Thousands still visit his bier to pay their respects to a frog that may have led the most extraordinary life of any lesser creature in history.

He was the star of an early sound motion picture. President Calvin Coolidge invited him to the White House. At the St. Louis Zoo, more than 40,000 people turned out in a single day to stare at him. He responded to their adulation by eating as many red ants as his visitors would feed him.

Old Rip had notoriety thrust upon him. Until July 19, 1897, he was a nameless horned lizard, a diminutive species of the iguana family. On that beautiful summer day, however, destiny was to smile on the lizard and he was to contribute a strange footnote to the history of Texas.

It was an historic day in Eastland. The town, with fewer than 1,000 residents, was the county seat and had been since 1875. On this day, the cornerstone was to be laid for a new county courthouse. There ceremonies were to include speeches by prominent citizens and a concert by the town band.

As E.E. Wood, a cornetist in the band, left home that morning to meet his colleagues on the town square, he noticed his little son sitting in the yard playing with a horned toad — a common pet of youngsters of that era. For some never explained reason, the musician picked up the toad and took him along to the ceremonies. That impulsive act was to start Old Rip on his road to fame.

Arriving at the square, Mr. Wood handed the toad to a friend and suggested that the creature be placed in the cornerstone just before it was sealed. The friend agreed, although neither could recall later why they thought it would contribute to posterity to entomb a live frog.

For the next thirty-one years, the cornerstone — with Old Rip in residence — remained in place. By 1928, however, the courthouse was in such need of major repair that the county commissioners declared it unsafe. They voted to demolish it and build another — the county's fifth seat of government — on the site.

Mr. Wood, still alive at the time, reminded officials that the horned toad's body (assuming that the vacuum and total darkness had preserved it) likely would be found when the cornerstone was opened. Others suggested that the toad just might have survived his three decades of imprisonment. The newspapers played the story for all its worth and, on February 18, 1928, when the cornerstone was to be opened, more than 2,000 people jammed the courthouse square.

The news story of the Eastland horned frog had gone around the world. Reporters from as far away as Dallas and Fort Worth, plus a correspondent for the Associated Press, were on hand for the cornerstone's opening. Television, of course, was still two decades away or else the networks probably would have had cameras on hand to record the events live.

Selected to oversee the opening and to make a report on the frog's condition to the assembled throng was a local citizen of unquestioned veracity, the Reverend R.E. Singleton, pastor of the Methodist Church. He watched closely as the bricks were pulled away and the concrete top of the cornerstone carefully broken with a hammer. As the seal was raised, the crowd stood in almost total silence.

Reverend Singleton then stepped to the open cornerstone, peered inside intently and then made the electrifying announcement: "There's the frog!"

Standing with him were a half dozen other Eastland men of impeccable reputation. They looked and verified Reverend

Singleton's word. Then the late Eugene Day, a prominent oil man of the time, reached into the opening and hauled out a very dirty, very flat horned toad. He passed the body on to Ed S. Prichard, the county judge and ranking official present. The judge gingerly took the toad by a hind leg and held him up for all to see.

Suddenly a woman screamed and the crowd gasped. The frog moved! Seconds later he opened his mouth, gulped a belly full of fresh air and swelled to his normal size. Then he blinked his eyes in a kind of wonderment. And from that moment on, he was a celebrity in Texas and all over the world.

There were doubters, of course. Renowned scientists argued in learned papers that it was impossible for any creature dependent on oxygen and food to sustain life could exist for thirty-one years in a sealed, airless environment. Others argued that such an existence might be possible for a creature of the desert known to be able to live for long periods without food or water. Texas experts were not among the skeptics; they were aware of the old Indian legend that members of the iguana family can live a century without any of the normal life supports.

At any rate, none of the witnesses present that day ever expressed any doubt that Old Rip was the same frog who had been placed in the cornerstone thirty-one years before. And since everybody wanted a close look at him, he was carted off to a local drugstore and placed in the window so that his new public could pay their respects.

There his first headline-making adventure happened. A few hours after he was put in a Roi-Tan cigar box and placed in the window, both the box and its occupant disappeared. Rumor had it that the celebrated frog had been kidnapped and an all-points bulletin was put out by the Eastland County sheriff. Sure enough, authorities in El Paso apprehended the kidnapper the next day and he and his victim were returned to Eastland.

No charges were filed, however. The county attorney couldn't decide what crime, if any, had been committed. Simple theft of a horned toad wasn't in the law books.

(It would be different today. The horned toad, once so prevalent that every Texas school boy carried one around in his pocket, is now a rare and endangered species. Just to have a toad in one's possession can mean a fine of $100 to $200. A second offense can bring a $500-$1,000 fine and from thirty to ninety days in jail, or both!)

Fortunately for Old Rip's career as a celebrity, however, possession of a horned toad was legal in 1928. Mr. Wood, who claimed ownership since he had contributed the creature to the cornerstone in the first place, believed that the entire nation should have an opportunity to meet Old Rip.

Newsreel companies, none of which had thought the opening of the courthouse cornerstone was a story worth their coverage, now converged on Eastland with cameras rolling. Robert L. Ripley, whose "Believe-It-or-Not" column was the most widely syndicated newspaper feature in the world at the time, gave Old Rip's story top billing.

Mr. Wood took him on tour. At the St. Louis Zoo, the crowds stood in line for hours to glimpse the West Texas frog with much the same enthusiasm people in Washington, New Orleans and wherenot responded to the exhibit of Egypt's King Tut artifacts in 1978. Old Rip was the star of the hour; so much so that a sound motion picture was produced around him when he visited New York.

His career reached its zenith, however, when the late Earle B. Mayfield, then U.S. Senator from Texas, arranged a meeting with President Coolidge. Coolidge insisted on hearing the full story of Old Rip's entombment from Mr. Wood as the toad sat on the presidential desk. "Silent Cal," never one to be overly friendly with visitors, stroked the horned toad's back and even asked about his diet.

After the White House visit, Mr. Wood and Old Rip returned to Eastland for a deserved rest. His new home was a goldfish bowl lined with sand and leaves in the Wood's parlor, an environment much superior to the cornerstone that had been his abode for so long. He spent most of his time catching up on his appetite, eating red ants by the dozen. Between meals he liked to burrow beneath the sand and nap.

For Old Rip, however, the good life was to be short. He was found dead on January 19, 1929, apparently the victim of the capricious West Texas winter. He had been relaxing in his glass house in a warm sun and had dozed off. A famed Texas "blue" norther hit unexpectedly, as they are wont to do sometimes, and the toad froze to death.

As befitting one of his standing in the community, Old

Rip's body was taken to an Eastland funeral home. There it lay in state while hundreds of the townspeople paid their respects.

When a national casket company heard of the tragedy, they offered to make a special glass coffin as Old Rip's last resting place. The offer was accepted and the box eventually was entombed atop a beautiful marble column in the lobby of the new Eastland County courthouse.

There Old Rip remains today, still visited by hundreds who come from everywhere to see the embalmed body of a horned toad whose only claim to fame was staying alive in an environment in which no other living creature could have survived.

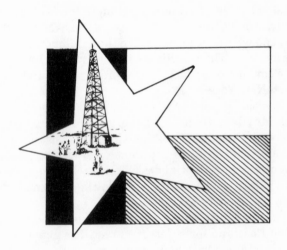

The $5 Million Picnic

In the world of oil, Edgar B. Davis, a Yankee-turned-Texan, is revered as the wildcatter who, against the advice of every expert, developed one of the state's most productive fields. In New York they still talk of him as the financial angel who spent $2 million backing a play so bad that tickets were offered free to anybody who would sit through it. But in Luling, Texas, his adopted home and site of his oil empire, he is remembered as the host who spent $5 million on a picnic and invited 30,000 guests.

A $5 million picnic? Even in today's inflationary economy, Davis's treat for his fellow townspeople ranks as the most expensive gala ever staged in a state noted for costly conviviality. It happened on June 11, 1926, and it celebrated the biggest oil deal in Texas up to that time — the sale of his field to Magnolia Petroleum for $12,100,000. Half was in cash and half was to come from the sale of oil, and Davis elected to spend most of the cash on his picnic.

Although Davis's lavish party lifted few eyebrows among the new millionaires who had struck it rich in Texas oil, it must have surprised his old friends in Brocktown, Massachusetts, where he had first proved his ability to make money. Descendant of one of the oldest New England families, Davis had reluctantly elected to forego a Harvard education to join his brother in the shoe manufacturing business. By the age of

Texas always has had more than its share of millionaires, but Edgar B. Davis is the only one who shared his wealth by staging the richest picnic in history.

—Photo from San Antonio *Express-News*

thirty-five, he had made his first million, suffered a nervous collapse and left on a long sea voyage to regain his health.

In Dutch Sumatra, he discovered rubber — a commodity he realized the U.S. must have in great supply as it entered the automobile age. A religious man who always felt that his every move was guided by a divine Providence, he decided that it was God's will that he develop this new industry. With $1 million of his own and support from American companies, he spent ten years in Sumatra laying out rubber plantations, improving production and preparing to put the world on wheels. Once he felt that he had completed his mission, he sold out his interests, returned to the United States and distributed more than $1 million of his profits as gifts to his associates and employees.

Although only forty-five, he considered retirement and bought an estate on the Massachusetts coast. A firm believer that the soul returned in another body after death, he commissioned an old high school classmate to write a play on the subject of reincarnation and induced Brock Pemberton to gather an expert cast and produce it on Broadway. Critics called it the worst drama ever produced, but Davis liked it and continued to keep "The Ladder" open by supplying free tickets to all comers. He finally closed it and went off to London hoping he could induce J. Arthur Rank to make a film of it at Davis's expense. Rank refused and "The Ladder" faded into oblivion.

Davis, however, did not. Back in Brocktown, his brother, Oscar, had invested $75,000 in oil leases in Caldwell County, Texas, and he asked Edgar to go down and have a look at the properties. And so, in 1921, he arrived in Luling — a stop on the Southern Pacific Railroad, which, more than four decades after its founding, was still only a village. It was situated on a geological area known as the Austin Chalk and most of the experts already had decided that the oil leases were worthless.

Edgar Davis, however, was never one to listen to the experts. Besides he again felt that Providence had sent him to Texas on a mission. Ignoring all advice to return to Massachusetts and forget any hope of finding oil, Davis bought his brother's leases and started drilling wells. He drilled six dry holes, using up all of the $1,500,000 left from his venture in rubber plantations after his gifts of much of his profits to his associates. Broke and despairing that the mystic message he had received from God might have been garbled in the transmission, Davis was finally ready to give up and return home.

Like a vision from Heaven, however, he suddenly remembered that he still had $80,000 in British bonds left from the Sumatra adventure and he decided to gamble it all on a seventh try. After the rig was set up, Davis discovered that he didn't have a clear title to the lease and decided to move it to the Rafael Rios farm. His geologist disagreed, arguing that it would be a waste of time to drill at the new location. However, Davis insisted and had the rig skidded a mile to the location that became known as the Rios Number 1.

It would be pleasant to record that the Rios Number 1 came in as a gusher and drenched Davis and his friends with the black gold. Indeed, some writers have reported that this is what happened. It makes a good story, but it isn't true. The Rios Number 1, destined to be the premier well of the Luling field, actually was brought in with only a trickle of oil.

On August 9, 1922 — which happened to be his mother's birthday — Davis drove out to the Rios Number 1. Because he was a believer in psychic phenomena, he felt that the day was of special significance and it was. When he arrived at the site, Drew Mosely, the driller, showed him a little oil seeping from the hole around the drill. K.C. Baker, the tool-pusher who had been associated with Davis in the rubber business in Sumatra, urged that the well be drilled deeper.

Mosely, wise in the ways of Texas oil, refused. He knew that drilling deeper would penetrate the salt water that lies under the Edwards Plateau — the same water that exerted pressure on the oil lying above it. To drill to a greater depth would have ruined the well. Mosely shut it down, directed the completion and allowed the oil to flow freely as the pressure built. And so the Rios Number 1 became a "gusher" in the sense that it was a highly productive well, but it never spewed oil over the derrick and onto bystanders as folklore has it.

It did, however, usher in the famous Luling field. And as Davis drilled ever more wells, some, indeed, were gushers in the real meaning of the word. On at least one occasion, Davis and two friends were literally drenched with oil as a new well came in. And all of the wells gushed millions into the pockets of the man who dreamed that his God-given mission was to find oil. Within twenty-five years, the discovery of Edgar B.

Davis had resulted in almost 100 million barrels of oil worth $135 million at 1947 prices.

By 1926, Davis was many times a millionaire when he made his deal with Magnolia to sell his field. At fifty-three, he had made three fortunes and was ready to retire. But unlike most people, Edgar Davis felt that his success had created a debt that he owed to his God and to those who had helped him to create his great wealth. He decided to repay these debts with a picnic the likes of which Texas has not seen since.

His own considerable lands in Caldwell County were filled with oil derricks, so he bought two sites just for the celebration. He purchased one hundred acres along the San Marcos River on which to stage the party for his white friends. On the other side of Luling, he bought forty acres as the site for the entertainment of his black friends.

Invitations by word of mouth and in writing went to everyone in Caldwell and Guadalupe Counties, to all of his former employees whom he could reach, to friends all over the world and to almost everybody else within traveling distance of Luling. He put up two electric *Welcome* signs, built dance floors at each site, brought in special entertainment from New York and two dance bands from San Antonio.

To feed his guests, he bought 12,200 pounds of beef, 5,180 pounds of lamb, 2,000 frying chickens, 28,800 bottles of soft drinks, 8,700 bricks of ice cream and another 85 gallons of this dessert, plus 7,000 cakes. And since virtually everybody smoked in this era before knowledge of lung cancer, he laid in 100,000 cigarettes and 7,500 cigars. Those who preferred chewing tobacco had to furnish their own.

The food and entertainment were lavish, but Davis wasn't through. Mounting the speaker's stand at each picnic, he quoted the admonition of Jesus: "What doth it profit a man if he shall gain the whole world and lose his own soul?" Then he announced that every member of his organization would share in his wealth. The five members of the management committee got $200,000 each. Every key worker received amounts up to $50,000. The 300 rank and file workers who had drilled his wells and got his product to market received bonuses of up to 100% of their total earnings, the percentage depending on how long they had been in Davis's employ.

Neither did he overlook Luling, the Texas country town

that had taken him in as a stranger and made him feel welcome. To the town he gave not one, but two, complete country clubs — one for its white citizens and one for its blacks. Club houses and golf courses were not enough, however, so he also provided an endowment for each so that no member would ever be charged dues. His final gift was another $1 million to establish a model farm to teach farmers how to diversify their crops.

When the picnics ended, Davis had spent $5 million. He said goodbye to Luling and to Texas and returned to Massachusetts to enjoy the great wealth he still had. After awhile, however, he returned to Luling again, started drilling more wells and developed another producing field. He suffered some financial losses, once almost was forced to declare bankruptcy but always seemed to recover his fiscal health.

On October 14, 1951, Edgar Davis suffered a stroke and fell from the porch of his home in Luling. Two days later, at age seventy-eight, he died. When he was buried in an oak grove adjoining the Luling Foundation which he had founded, pastors from every church in town participated in the services. Most of the townspeople turned out for the last rites for their friend who, twenty-five years before, had hosted the picnic that Luling, and all of Texas, won't soon forget.

Port Arthur:
The City the Brownies Built

Today's visitor to Port Arthur would be hard put to find anything supernatural about this bustling Gulf port city of more than 60,000 mortals.

Its oil refineries, petrochemical plants and loading docks have helped to make it the nation's ninth largest ocean port. Yet it might have remained an alligator-infested swamp seven miles from deep water if creatures from the spirit world had not intervened.

Arthur Edward Stilwell, the entrepreneur the spirits chose as their worldly agent, referred to them as his "brownies" in private conversation. Acting on their advice, he founded not only Port Arthur but thirty-eight other towns and villages in three states, colonized 600,000 acres of Texas land and amassed a fortune of more than $160 million.

Stilwell was a hard-headed businessman, not a spiritualist. Born in 1859 into a well-to-do Rochester, New York, family, he was the son of a physician and grandson of the city's mayor. When, at age fifteen, family financial problems forced him to end his education and go to work, he began to be guided by "hunches" — advice which he said came to him from "brownies" from the spirit world.

From the beginning, their counsel directed him to success in almost everything he undertook. When they advised him to become a printer, he did. By the time he was eighteen, his "brownies" had put him in the railroad business, albeit by the back door. He got a contract to print 5,000 timetables each

127

month for a Virginia short line and soon was performing the same service for several others. As a teenager he found himself netting $2,000 a week at a time when every dollar was worth 100 cents.

Three years earlier, his advisors from the spirit world had given him his life goal: to build a railroad from the middle of the United States to the Gulf of Mexico. They also had predicted that he would find and marry a Virginia beauty when he was nineteen. The second prediction came true when he met Jennie Wood in Virginia when he had just turned nineteen, married her and moved to Chicago.

For awhile it appeared that his brownies had been wrong. Stilwell found no opportunities in railroading and became an insurance agent. Soon he had topped every agent the company had in the country in sales and also had created two new insurance policies. These were so innovative that his company and two others paid him handsomely for the right to sell them. Young Stilwell pocketed the profits and moved south to Kansas City.

Building a railroad required lots of capital, so Stilwell's brownies led him to establish a vehicle to provide it. He organized the Missouri, Kansas and Texas Trust Company in 1886 to do just that. Shortly after he met E.L. Martin, a wealthy businessman and former Kansas City mayor. Martin dreamed of building a belt railroad around the city. He asked Stilwell, then twenty-five, to use his trust company to raise the money.

Martin's appeal to Stilwell was a last resort. He had tried to raise money for the venture for many months with no success. Then on a Tuesday in October, 1887, Martin approached Stilwell. He told him that his franchise to build the line would expire the following Friday and that the opportunity would be lost if work couldn't start within seventy-two hours. At least $350,000 was needed to start construction.

As Stilwell listened, his brownies provided him with a "hunch" that he could raise the needed money. He hadn't the slightest idea how he would do it, but he told Martin to have a contractor standing by to start work Friday morning. Then the two boarded a train for Philadelphia to seek investors.

"My companion would have been less than optimistic if he had known that I was simply following a hunch," Stilwell wrote later.

As usual, however, the brownies were right. Stilwell got the needed capital and construction of the railroad began. He envisioned much more than just a belt line around the city, however. He saw the line being built on to the Gulf to a port that would accommodate ocean-going ships. The vision came closer to reality in 1891 when, at age thirty-two, he was named president of the railroad. In 1893, he reorganized it as the Kansas City, Pittsburg & Gulf and started aiming his tracks south.

Stilwell chose Shreveport, Louisiana, as his first southern terminus. Raising capital was difficult, however, because of the depression of 1893. But his brownies had an answer. They told him to go to Holland for investors.

He knew only one Dutchman, a coffee broker named John DeGeoijen. As soon as Stilwell outlined his plan, however, DeGeoijen agreed to become his representative in Holland. Soon Dutchmen from all walks of life were buying bonds in Stilwell's railroad. Investors included Queen Wilhelmina herself. (Later Stilwell would name two of the stations on his line, Mena and DeQueen in Arkansas, in gratitude to her royal highness.)

With the completion of the line from Kansas City to Shreveport assured, Stilwell's plan was to buy a railroad connecting the Louisiana city with Houston and Galveston. However, his brownies entered the picture at this point and advised against this course.

"Galveston will soon be destroyed by a storm," Stilwell wrote that the spirits told him. "Build a new railroad directly southward from Shreveport through the virgin forests and locate your Texas terminal on the north shore of Sabine Lake."

Stilwell's hunch from his supernatural advisors was even more specific. They pictured for him a city of 100,000 on the north bank of Lake Sabine "which could be connected with the Gulf by means of a canal about seven miles long. Here, in this landlocked harbor, safe from the most devastating storm the Gulf could produce, we would erect elevators and piers and create a port for the shipment of the Western farmers' export grain."

And the city would be called Port Arthur.

When Stilwell told his directors of his change in plans, they could only stare in disbelief. The area was swampland, filled with alligators and worth less than $7 an acre. The plan for the new terminus was approved, however, and in 1895, the railroad acquired more than 46,000 acres of uninhabited swamp and announced that the city of Port Arthur would be built.

It wasn't easy. Although the townsite company laid out 6,000 lots and donated considerable land for schools, parks and churches, few residents flocked to Stilwell's dream city. The railroad built a luxury hotel, erected a pleasure pier in the lake and built a natatorium as a tourist attraction. Two years after the townsite was laid out, however, there were fewer than 70 residents. By the fall of 1897, things began to look up and an early census listed a population of 860 and sixteen business houses.

Without a canal connecting Port Arthur with the Gulf, however, neither the railroad nor the town could survive. Again Stilwell's brownies came to his aid with explicit instructions on how such a canal should be built.

"Build the canal with the same width at the top and the same width at the bottom and the same depth as the Suez Canal," they told him. "Dig it on the west shore of Sabine Lake and put earth on the east bank to protect the canal from any storm."

The advice from the spirits may have come easy to Stilwell, but implementing it did not. The project was too costly for the railroad to undertake without government help. Landowners in the area opposed it and filed dozens of lawsuits to try and stop it. Stilwell and the railroad won in the end, but all of his companies were bankrupt. The final blow came when the stockholders of the railroad put the line in receivership and removed Stilwell from the management.

Neither Stilwell nor his brownies were through, however. Next they turned their attention to a new idea for a railroad. To be called the Kansas City, Mexico and Orient, it would run from the midwest terminal to a new city on the gulf of California and that city would be called Port Stilwell.

Stilwell's spirit advisors were confident that a railroad across West Texas to Presidio, then across the border to Mexico and on to Topolobampo would make money. They assured him that: "Within two years, a great oil field will spring up along the route."

The Orient, as the road came to be known, was slowly built through West Texas as far as Alpine. But a drouth, crop failures and revolution in Mexico forced the line into bankruptcy before it reached the border. However, the spirits had been right: In 1923, the Big Lake oil field was brought in near San Angelo and prosperity returned. Eventually Stilwell's dream of a railroad to the west coast of Mexico was completed, but by others.

The Brownies were right about Port Arthur, too. In 1900, Galveston was hit by the great hurricane that killed more than 6,000 and left the city devastated. Port Arthur was untouched. And a few months later, only sixteen miles from the terminal Stilwell built and named for himself, the famous Lucas gusher was brought in at Spindletop and one of the world's great oil fields was underway.

Stilwell and his hunches that he got from his brownies had been right all along. Only their timing had been wrong. And their dreams, whether they originated in the world of the supernatural or in the fertile mind of a man ahead of his time, have all come true.

Arthur Edward Stilwell, who died in New York in 1928, would have liked that.

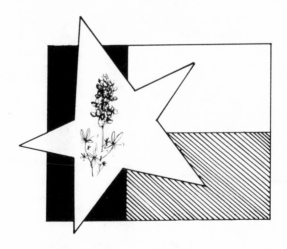

He doesn't look like a fighter, but thirty million just like him were drafted from a single Texas county in World War II as a secret weapon against Japan.

—Photo from the San Antonio *Express-News*

The Batty Bombers

In Ney Cave, deep inside the fence lines of a Bandera County ranch, reside the lineal descendants of one of the most unique attack forces ever to take the field of battle.

The cave dwellers are *Tadarida mexicana* — Mexican free-tailed bats, in the common parlance — and an estimated 30 million of them call the cavern home. Small, brown, broad-eared creatures with very narrow, pointed wings, they are peaceful by nature, rarely attacking anything except mosquitoes which they devour by the thousands. Yet for a period during World War II, the ancestors of these Texas bats provided a secret weapon which U. S. Navy strategists believed would help America win its struggle with Japan.

On paper, at least, the tactical assignment to the bats sounded simple: They were to carry tiny incendiary bombs into the very heart of Tokyo and cause thousands of fires that would level the Japanese capital.

The idea was not as preposterous as it sounds. The Mexican free-tail is the swift of the bat world. They emerge each twilight from their cave, swoop almost to the ground and then take off skyward like a fighter plane on a mission. Although they prefer the darkness, they fly either night or day with astonishing precision by sonar, a marvel of miniaturization that is more complex and sophisticated than any yet devised by man. In fact, scientists are carefully studying the bat's acousti-

133

cal system and its other mechanisms to see if machines can duplicate them for the benefit of mankind.

Thus Mexican free-tail is a superb flying machine that is able to out maneuver the most sophisticated airplane ever built. And in 1944, when jet power and computerization were still in the future, the little bat with the mouse-like tail seemed to the military to be the living, breathing answer to the problem of penetrating Japan's anti-aircraft defenses.

The Navy's plan to draft Texas bats into the service of the country's military establishment had some precedent, too. Some eighty years earlier, the four-inch long creatures with the bewhiskered face and broad, leather-like ears were mustered into noncombat service in the Civil War by the Army of the Confederacy. What the South wanted was not the bats, but their guano — the droppings they leave behind after feasting on mosquitoes.

Bat guano has a very high nitrogen content and nitrogen is a key ingredient in the manufacture of gunpowder. When Federal gunboats succeeded in blockading Gulf ports early in the war, the South's supply of niter was cut off and munitions manufacture all but stopped. Then somebody discovered a limitless supply of nitrogen in Texas bat caves and regiments of Blue and Gray troops moved into several to guard this important source of materiel.

Once the war ended, the bats were allowed to continue their production of guano in peace, but not for long. Nitrogen also happens to be one of the world's most desirable fertilizers and the recovery and sale of guano became a lucrative business. If bat guano wasn't worth its weight in gold, it was worth a lot of dollars in the market place. Texas bat caves (and there are about a dozen which produce guano in commercial quantities) became valuable pieces of real estate.

In time, the manure dropped by the bats was bringing $60 a ton as fertilizer. After some sharp dealers assured themselves a magnificent retirement by mining 100,000 tons of the stuff out of the Carlsbad Caverns, some even sharper promoters decided it was time to domesticate the Mexican free-tails and put the production of guano on an assembly line basis.

Though the tiny bats seem to prefer caverns as roosting places, they often take up residence in vacant buildings or any relatively dark, dry retreat. The one requirement is that they have plenty of neighbors and one of the reasons the bats may prefer caves is because a large cavern can accommodate millions of their kind. Their other necessity is an accessible supply of mosquitoes. So, reasoned the promoters, if one could provide the bats with a dark, dry apartment and lots of the stinging insects, almost anybody could produce guano in his own backyard.

This, of course, would require having one's own "bat tower" — a contraption twenty feet high, twelve feet square at the base and six feet square at the top. These towers, each complete with a colony of bats, could be purchased at a price from the developers of the idea.

The rest was easy, according to the sales brochure. That prospectus, aptly titled "Bats, Mosquitoes and Dollars," pointed out that all the owner of a bat tower had to do was to wait a bit. Once the inhabitants of the tower had had time to convert the mosquitoes into liquid gold through the alchemy of digestion, the investor needed only to empty the guano occasionally (a special chute was built into the tower for that purpose) and exchange it for dollars in a fertilizer-hungry world.

The bats, however, rebelled at being treated like laying hens and deserted the man-made towers for residences of their own choice. Apparently the promoters thought that the bats would be unable to navigate any distance from the installation and would be forced to return to it after each foray for food. It wasn't until much later that naturalists discovered that the Mexican free-tail is not restricted by geography. Bats from Central Texas caves sometimes fly to the Gulf of Mexico if choice mosquitoes are swarming on the beaches, then return to their home caverns. This is round trip flight of up to 300 miles!

This ability to fly long distances was one of the reasons the Mexican free-tail was recruited by the Navy in World War II. Another was the bat's unique ability to awaken from the deep sleep of hibernation within a few seconds. A third was the creature's diminutive size. Navy strategists assumed that no Japanese would suspect that these tiny things actually were invaders sent by the enemy to destroy a city.

"Project X-Ray," as the plan was called, began in 1944 when the Navy leased Ney Cave, thirty miles northwest of Hondo, and took over the supervision of its thirty million residents. The idea was to equip each bat selected for the mission with a tiny incendiary bomb strapped to its chest.

Once the bombs were in place, the bats were put in crates and refrigerated at 40 degrees Fahrenheit — cold enough to send them into hibernation. Later the plan was to drop the crates of sleeping bats over a wide area of Tokyo. Coming out of hibernation as they dropped into warmer temperatures, the bats would take refuge in the nearest building on landing. And since the Tokyo of 1944 was mostly a city of flimsy wood and bamboo structures, almost anywhere a bat landed would be a possible spot for these airborne arsonists.

The Navy had it all figured to the last detail. The little incendiary bombs were triggered by the temperature. Once either the bat's body warmth or the atmosphere reached 80 degrees, the bomb would begin to burn. And with thousands of bomb-laden bats strategically placed throughout the Japanese capital, the Navy predicted the greatest conflagration since the burning of ancient Rome.

It didn't happen that way. As arsonists, the bats from Texas produced no damage in Tokyo beyond dropping some guano. A bomb bay load of the little invaders, each armed with a supposedly fool-proof incendiary, was dropped on the Japanese capital. Not even a grass fire resulted.

The Mexican free-tails that were involved in the Navy's unusual experiment are all gone now. The lifetime of the little bat is only about twenty years (equal to 200 years for a man). But their descendants live on at Ney Cave and dozens of other caverns in the state. Except for producing guano and keeping the Texas mosquito population in check, the bats haven't contributed much either to society or to history since they failed to win World War II.

But who knows? There are military experts who still regard these tiny creatures as a potentially useful weapon in America's arsenal. The bat bombers of Texas may someday fly again.

The Seventh Flag Over Texas

Don't believe the history books' brag that six flags have flown over Texas. Historians don't always tell the whole story. In the matter of national standards flitting in the Texas breeze, the historians either can't count or else have chosen to ignore a second independent "republic" that existed within these borders for eleven short months.

It all started on the streets of Laredo, hard by the Rio Grande. Since 1775, when Tomas Sanchez de la Barrera y Gallardo started his own town on the site, Laredo has been a favorite destination of tourists and a popular meeting place for small conventions. It was one of those conventions that was to found a new nation and give Texas its seventh flag.

Sanchez, an ex-soldier turned frontier rancher, had no aspirations to be remembered by history when he asked the King of Spain to grant him fifteen leagues of sand and mesquite so he could start a town of his own. Apparently his only interest in founding a settlement was to get himself elected mayor, or *alcalde*. When he settled his family and a contingent of ranch hands on the Rio Grande on May 15, 1775, and proclaimed that the site henceforth would be called "Laredo," he had no idea that he was founding the capital city of a new nation.

Unfortunately, Sanchez didn't live to see that happen. When he died in 1796, Mexico was still a province of Spain, Texas was a part of Mexico and the peasants were reasonably

The capitol of a Republic that lasted only eleven months still stands in Laredo.

—Photo from the U.T. Institute of Texan Cultures

content. Independence for Mexico was still in the future and the Republic of Texas wasn't even a dream. Neither had anyone yet conceived the idea for still a third nation which, although short-lived, would be remembered as the Republic of the Rio Grande with Sanchez's town, Laredo, its seat of government.

By 1822, the citizens of Mexico had divorced themselves from the rule of Spain and the new government had set about to build a new nationalism. As with all new and developing nations, however, there were problems, not the least of which was half of a state known as Coahuila and Texas. By 1835, when Antonio Lopez de Santa Anna, an army officer committed to a strong central government, ascended to the presidency of Mexico and established himself as dictator, the Texas half of Coahuila and Texas declared its independence. After losing at the Alamo and winning handily at San Jacinto, Texas became a free and independent republic. The date was April 21, 1836.

Mexico's problems were far from over, however. There were many leaders, particularly in the northern states of the country, who were strong federalists and opposed to the centralist policies of the Santa Anna government. One of these was a lawyer named Antonio Canales.

Canales was a pretty good lawyer, but his real ambition was to be a general. If he had stayed in his law office instead of testing his military genius (of which he had almost none), he probably would have been remembered only as a successful small-town lawyer. As it turned out, his role in history is that of a comic opera general who lost the battle and the war as well as the dream of establishing a new nation within the Republic of Texas.

As early as 1835, federalist leaders in Tamaulipas, Nuevo Leon and Coahuila had attempted to force Mexico to return to the Constitution of 1824 which gave less power to the central government. Failing in that enterprise, they were nevertheless heartened by the success of Texas in winning *de facto* independence. In all probability, Texas's success influenced their efforts to win freedom also.

At any rate, the federalists in the northern tier of Mexican states looked around for a convivial site to meet and decide on their future plans. They settled on Laredo, by now a thriving city of more than 1,700 and already offering many of the amenities visitors have come to expect along the Texas border. They gathered there on January 17, 1840 for the first political convention ever held on the Rio Grande.

There they declared their intention to establish the Republic of the Rio Grande and elected one Jesus de Cardenas as president. Lawyer Canales realized his ambition when he was named commander-in-chief of the Republic's non-existent (at least, at that time) army. However, the delegates to the convention promised to conscript one, and within a couple of months, General Canales was ready to do battle.

Meanwhile, the new Republic of the Rio Grande had to have a capitol. It found one in the tiny adobe building on San Agustin Plaza that had been used by the Spanish government. That building, still standing alongside the posh La Posada Hotel on Zaragoza Street, was to be the seat of government until the new Republic went down in defeat.

Since Texas had won independence on the battlefield, Canales felt that his government's road to freedom led to an immediate confrontation with the centralist forces. On March 24–25, 1840, he led his motley army to war at Morales, Coahuila. It was a disaster. Not only was his force routed, but Canales's cavalry commander and principal advisor, Colonel Antonio Zapata, was captured and executed.

What was left of the army of the Republic of the Rio Grande retreated back across the river. General Canales, however, apparently felt that retreat was the better part of valor and ordered his force to keep marching north. They didn't stop until they reached San Antonio, 150 arid miles from their capital city.

At least, they were a long way from what had been their capital. As a precaution against attack from the Mexican centralists, the government also fled north to temporary quarters in Texas at Victoria. Once the government was relocated and the army was relaxing in San Antonio, the commander-in-chief decided to go to Austin and try to get some help.

In April, 1840, Canales arrived in Austin and got an appointment with President Mirabeau B. Lamar of the Republic of Texas. Lamar, although very much in sympathy with any group seeking to get out from under Mexican rule, refused any firm offer to help. Texas, after all, was still negotiating in an effort to get Mexico to recognize the new independent republic and Lamar was enough of a diplomat to know that Santa Anna's government would not be pleased to hear that he was helping three other Mexican states win their freedom.

Canales was not easily discouraged, however, so he rode out of Austin toward Houston. There he was well received, picked up some financial support and some recruits for his rag tag army and then went on to San Patricio. In that Irish settlement not far from Victoria, he discovered that his fighting force had grown to 300 Mexicans, 140 Americans and 80 Indians and the number was increasing daily. Best of all, the Americans had a leader — Colonel Sam W. Jordan, a veteran of the Texan Army.

Jordan was a depression-ridden soldier of fortune who, only a few months later, would try to kill Sam Houston with an axe. But he was the only one of Canales's force who knew anything about combat. The commander-in-chief was so elated to have a trained fighting man around that he dispatched Jordan and ninety men toward the Rio Grande.

Although he obviously was mentally ill and was to end his life as a suicide, Jordan was a brilliant field commander. He led the army of the Republic of the Rio Grande into the interior of Tamaulipas and captured Ciudad Victoria without a battle. Some of his subordinate officers turned out to be spies for Mexico, however, and they urged him to march toward San Luis Potosi where they knew the little army would be annihilated. Jordan discovered their treachery early on and turned his force toward Saltillo.

There, on October 25, 1840, he was attacked by the centralist army. Although some of his command had defected, Jordan managed to defend himself and get most of his troops back to the comparative safety of Texas. By November, however, Canales realized that he was fighting a lost cause and he capitulated. He was taken into the centralist army as an officer and federalism in Mexico was dead. So was the Republic of the Rio Grande.

The idea of a second nation within Texas did not die, however. In 1954, some South Texas business leaders met again in Laredo in convention assembled. They discussed seceding from the United States (and Texas) and reorganizing the Republic of the Rio Grande with twenty Texas counties that are presently in the territory claimed by that government. They wrote a "constitution" which called for no income taxes, bull fighting, open gambling and allowed a number of other freedoms.

It was all a joke, of course. But in Laredo, the Republic of the Rio Grande is not. It still lives, in a sense, in the building where its government was headquartered. The little adobe building, freshly whitewashed, is now a museum. And over its entrance, seven flags are flown.

They are the standards of Spain, France, Mexico, the Lone Star of Texas, the United States and the Confederate States of America. The seventh flag, still flying proudly with the other six, is that of the Republic of the Rio Grande.

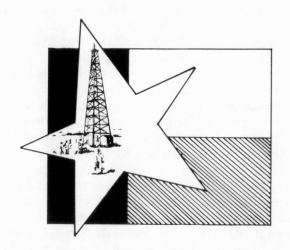

When The Earth Fell In

There are those who still live in the great pine and palmetto forests of Hardin County's "Big Thicket" who insist that it was the Devil himself who made the earth fall in. Satan, they say, was infuriated because greedy earthlings were stealing the fuel from the fires of Hell. To get even, he caused an entire producing oil field to sink into oblivion over three memorable days in October, 1929.

The swallowing of five acres of the Sour Lake Oil field by a disturbed earth was not the first diabolical prank to be played on Hardin County. Twenty years before a similar thing had happened in the old, and smaller, Batson Field. One day in 1909 a single wooden derrick, plus all of the equipment around it, disappeared into a hole that suddenly yawned in the ground. Workers decided that it was caused by a flowing well which had been brought in through a broken casing. When the rest of the area remained stable, they dismissed the incident and went ahead putting down more oil wells.

However, it was a different story two decades later at Sour Lake. And while scientists don't accept the theory that sorcery was involved, they acknowledge that the old-timers were correct in one sense. Only their conclusion was wrong. At the time of the incident, more than 100 million barrels of petroleum had been pumped from the Sour Lake field. While this may not have deprived Lucifer of fuel needed in Hades, it did play havoc with geological formations undergirding that part of Texas. Once the oil had been removed, there was no place for the topsoil and uppercrust to go but down. Thus it was Mother Nature, not the Devil, who rebelled against man's tampering with the Earth's underbelly.

Sour Lake, eighteen miles west of Beaumont, sits atop a giant salt dome that has produced both hot mineral springs and oil since before recorded history. For centuries Indians came to the natural lake to bathe in the sulphur waters that feed it and to gather the pitch that seeped through the earth around its shores. The first white settlers arrived in 1835, named the place Sour Lake Springs because of the odiferous waters and began developing it into a health resort. From the 1850s until the turn of the century, it was a favorite spa that attracted notables like Sam Houston, who believed the mud baths and mineral waters improved health.

In 1866, however, L.T. Barrett drilled the first commercially successful oil well at Oil Springs, some one hundred and twenty-five miles north of Sour Lake, and changed the economic history of Texas for all time to come. His venture set off a state-wide search for the liquid gold and, in 1902, a gusher was brought in outside of Sour Lake Springs. This was the beginning of a boom that was to end the community's days as a resort and make it an oil center. The new field was to create one giant company, Texaco, and see as many as 50,000 barrels of oil produced each day.

The most active drilling area was outside the town limits of Sour Lake at a place called Shoe String, so named because so many of the early wildcatters operated on a financial "shoestring." It was here on the morning of October 7, 1929, that workers got their first hint that something was amiss. Two wells owned by Texaco suddenly started pumping water instead of oil. To compound the mystery, several water wells in the area began producing petroleum.

By the next morning, it was obvious that the problem was serious. When the crew arrived for work at the two wells, there was an area only 100 feet away which wasn't there anymore. A space 100 by 150 feet had begun sinking and continued to drop slowly into the bowels of the earth. As it was pulled downward, the depression thus created filled with hot mineral water. By nightfall the subsidence was an estimated thirty feet deep and still dropping.

By the second day the depression was sixty feet deep and the affected area had started to widen. Large trees and oil derricks began to topple into the sinkhole and nearby buildings began to teeter on their foundations. The strange phenomenon began to attract crowds of spectators but curiosity turned to panic as tubing snapped on the wells near the depression and the earth seemed to shake.

Despite the danger, however, schools were dismissed in Sour Lake and Beaumont so the students could rush to the site and watch the earth fall in. Before the ground finally stopped moving, an estimated 20,000 people had come to watch and hundreds of others were en route from all over Texas.

By the time the subsidence had reached a depth of 160 feet, large cracks had formed in all directions from the site. Derricks on wells being drilled within 1,500 feet of the sinkhole were thrown out of line, their tubing twisted or broken at depths of between 450- and 525-feet. Oil and thick, sulphurous water poured through the cracks and the depression, forming a body of water that is still known today as Cavity Lake.

Before the earth stopped moving, a large powerhouse on the edge of the depression had rolled into the cavity and disappeared forever. One well which had never produced more than ten barrels of oil per day suddenly began spouting 250 barrels. However, thirty-five producing wells were knocked out of action entirely and none was ever restored to production. Altogether five acres of one of Texas's largest oil fields was swallowed up by the angry earth.

After seventy-two hours of slowly sinking, the subsidence stopped as abruptly as it had begun. By then a small army of geologists and other experts had moved in to try to determine why it had happened in the first place. They studied the area carefully, made all sorts of calculations and finally agreed that a number of factors might have caused the earth to fall in.

One theory was that a huge underground cavity was created in the series of salt domes on which Sour Lake sits. For almost three decades, these natural domes had been milked of the millions of barrels of oil they once contained and on which the earth's crust actually floated. With this liquid support gone, there was no place for the topsoil to sit and it eventually cracked and disappeared into the hole.

Some of the experts said that the area had an unstable geological formation and probably should never have been drilled for oil in the first place. Others contended that heavy blasting in the field had dislodged some rock formations and caused the earth's crust to sink. One scientist believed that it was water, not oil, which had dissolved the salt in the dome and created the cavity.

Veterans of the oil patch, although surprised by the extent of the sinking at Sour Lake, know that such sink holes are not too uncommon and that they are likely to happen again. Nor is it always the taking of oil that causes them. Grand Saline, in Van Zandt County, is a case in point. This area of East Texas is the largest producer of salt in the U. S. The product is produced both from underground mines and from wells fed by saline beds that extend over a thirty-square-mile area. From time to time, the earth, its support taken away by the removal of the salt, has been swallowed up in the resulting cavity.

The problems of disappearing earth is not limited to Texas, either. Federal Highway Administration officials, in a study made a few years back, suggested that fifteen percent of the entire country is in some danger of being swallowed up. These danger spots are in limestone regions where the rock has been leached out in honeycombs and filled with soil that floats on underground water. When the subterranean water level is lowered, the pressure cracks the thin rocks and the structure collapses inward.

Similar sinking has been recorded over the years at several points in Texas and others can happen in the future if the experts are correct. In Sour Lake, however, no further disturbances in the surface of the earth have been noted except for some sidewalks that have sunk several inches. The depression which swallowed up an entire oil field is now a local tourist attraction.

However, to some still resident in Sour Lake, the name of the cavity created by the 1929 sinking is a misnomer. They say that it should be called Lucifer's Lake as a kind of peace offering to the Devil who is still angry because the oil taken from the earth that once covered the waters caused the fires of Hell to sputter and die. Still others argue that Satan, if he did cause the problem, has forgiven the human race its frailty and greed. They point out that the Sour Lake field is still producing oil today.

Not a drop, however, comes from the area where the earth fell in.

Lieutenant Benjamin D. Foulois, America's first military pilot, is pictured with the Wright Type A biplane he used to launch for what now is the U.S. Air Force. This picture was made in 1911 at Eagle Pass after he had flown from San Antonio to set a new world record for distance flying!

—Courtesy Fort Sam Houston Military Museum, San Antonio

Even the U.S. Air Force Started Here

It was on the infantry parade ground of San Antonio's Fort Sam Houston that the military might of America ceased to be earthbound. On March 2, 1910, at precisely 9:30 a.m., a short, slight Signal Corps first lieutenant, Benjamin D. Foulois, lifted a Wright Type "A" biplane off the dirt to send the U. S. war machine sputtering into the wild blue yonder.

It was no accident that Foulois, a career soldier who had enlisted in the infantry and served a previous hitch in the cavalry, was destined to be the nation's first military pilot. His superiors selected him for three valid reasons:

1. He had taken a correspondence course in flying;

2. He had flown fifty-four minutes with Wilbur Wright, one of the brothers who invented the airplane, and 128 minutes with another pilot, and

3. At five feet, five inches in height and weighing only 135 pounds in his G. I. underwear, he probably was the smallest man in the Army.

Neither was he an unwilling test pilot. Starting as a private in the infantry, he had received his commission in 1901 and seemed destined to a career of commanding foot soldiers. However, when he read of early experiments by aviation pioneers, he asked for a transfer to the Signal Corps since that branch of the Army was doing some aerial experiments with balloons. Foulois (pronounced "fa-loy") concluded that his future with the military was in the air.

At Fort Leavenworth, Kansas, where he was sent for basic

Signal Corps training, he became more convinced than ever that the future military superiority of this country was in aviation. As a class assignment, he wrote a report on "The Tactical and Strategic Value of Dirigible Balloons and Aerodynamical Flying Machines." He predicted that such instruments of war would one day be used in aerial battles, for communication between ground units, for reconnaissance and even for photography.

To a world in which the first powered flight was barely five years old, Foulois's predictions sounded like something out of Jules Verne. His classmates and instructors at Fort Leavenworth put him down as a crank and his report was filed away and forgotten.

A similar fate might also have befallen military aviation except for the fact that the brothers Wright had wrecked one of the airplanes they had built. When they offered the pieces to the government for $1,500, some far-sighted army officer decided not to pass up the bargain.

U.S. *Aeroplane Number 1*, a far cry from the huge *Air Force One* jet used today by the President of the United States, arrived in San Antonio in seventeen boxes. It was received at the offices of Wells Fargo & Company, express agents, on February 3, 1910. The invoice of the bill of lading recorded the total weight of parts as 4,468 pounds.

Lieutenant Foulois arrived in San Antonio four days later on *The Katy Flyer*, then the fastest transport available. He had been ordered by General James Allen, chief of the Signal Corps, to go to Texas, "take plenty of spare parts with you, and teach yourself to fly." Apparently the general also warned him that he would have to assemble the flying machine himself because he brought a contingent of eight enlisted men with him.

In anticipation of momentous events to come, the commanding officer of Fort Sam Houston had ordered a shed measuring forty-nine by forty-one feet built on the northeast corner of the parade ground known as Arthur MacArthur Field (named for the father of General Douglas MacArthur and one-time commander of the fort). The Army called the building a "shed": actually it was to be the first hangar for military aircraft ever built in this country.

It took almost a month to get the structure finished and for Foulois to complete his plans. March 1 had been set as the target date and the young lieutenant arrived early that morning preparing to get the frail craft airborne. Since the little airplane had no wheels and was mounted on skids, it had to be launched by a catapult mechanism. When it was discovered that the belt supporting the pulley which hung from the catapult tower was not strong enough to sustain the heavy weights essential to the launch, the flight had to be postponed.

Foulois's ground crews worked all day correcting this problem. By the morning of March 2, however, the launching system was in operation and the pilot arrived at the field a little after 9 a.m. The day had dawned clear and almost perfect for flying and Foulois seated himself in the pilot's seat twenty minutes later. At precisely 9:30 a.m., he waved both arms as a signal for takeoff and the Wright *Flyer* was catapulted along a fifty-foot monorail and into the air.

"It rose without a bobble and sailed easily and majestically across the parade grounds," an observer told reporters later. (Strangely enough, no newspaper writers were on hand to record this historic event. Except for military personnel, few others watched Foulois's first flight.)

It must have been a thrilling moment for the handful of onlookers. The tiny plane, its 30-horsepower engine pumping, circled the field six times, going faster with each revolution and attaining the unheard of speed of fifty miles an hour. For almost seven minutes, Lieutenant Foulois kept the fragile craft aloft.

However, the first flight in military aviation history almost ended in disaster. As Foulois started to land on the south side of the field, he saw an automobile driven by Dr. L.L. Shropshire, a prominent San Antonio physician, heading directly toward him. Thinking quickly, the new pilot lifted the craft over the amazed motorist and landed a half mile farther than he had intended.

By that time, a crowd estimated at 300 had rushed to the outskirts of town to see the phenomenon of manned flight. When Foulois landed, he was engulfed by soldiers and civilians alike. He wasted little time on the plaudits of the crowd, however. He had planned at least four more flights that day and he insisted that the field be cleared.

He made another flight before lunch. When he landed the second time, the crowd had grown to thousands. A great cheer arose from the spectators and one newspaper reported that "with all the auto horns blowing, the noise was deafening." Lieutenant Foulois acknowledged the accolades with a wave and went to lunch at the Fort Sam Officers Mess.

After lunch and a brief rest, the pilot was back on the field to try again. The third flight was uneventful, but on the fourth, he ran into trouble. After twenty-one minutes, the fuel line broke and the little biplane plummeted like a rock from an altitude of about forty feet. Foulois emerged without a scratch but the plane's rudder was broken and the pilot had to hold on to keep from being tossed from the plane.

This incident resulted in an invention by the pilot that has become a national institution — the seat belt. Foulois didn't like the idea of being tossed about in the event of a crash. On his next flight, he secured himself in the pilot's seat with a four-foot leather strap he had removed from his trunk. Foulois's "safety belt" one day would become standard equipment in every airplane and in every auto sold in the U. S.

Before he could try out his new invention, however, the airplane had to be repaired. Putting it back in shape cost $300, a sum Lieutenant Foulois was obliged to pay out of his own pocket. Years later he liked to recall that the government had never reimbursed him for this expense.

Those first four flights over the Alamo City convinced Foulois that the airplane would never be a success as a military weapon so long as it depended on skids and a catapult to launch it. He suggested that the skids be replaced by wheels — an innovation credited with having a major role in the development of aviation.

That day in San Antonio when Foulois launched the Air Force was to have a salutary effect on his own career. He continued to fly the repaired Wright Type "A" for another four months, setting new world aviation distance and speed records almost each time he went up. Then, in May, 1911, Lieutenant George E.M. Kelly, who had trained with Foulois, was killed in a flying accident over Fort Sam Houston. The Signal Corps summarily ordered all flights from the parade grounds stopped.

Aviation, however, was a reality which the military could no longer ignore. The operation was moved to Maryland after Kelly's crash but only for a three-year period. The weather in

South Texas, "where the sunshine spends the winter," couldn't be ignored. The flight operations were moved back to Fort Sam Houston in 1914. A year later, Foulois, now wearing the bars of a captain, was sent back to Texas to organize an aviation post. He was given a fleet of six airplanes to command.

Foulois's 1st Aero Squadron, the first ever sent into combat by the U.S., was ordered to the border to assist General John J. Pershing in the punitive expedition against Mexico. While flying dispatches from Pershing to the American consul at Chihuahua, he and his copilot were arrested and held for a time in jail by Mexican authorities.

Pershing admired Foulois and was an advocate of expanding military aviation. When the United States entered World War I and Pershing was made Commander of the American Expeditionary Force, he saw to it that Foulois was promoted to brigadier general and made Chief of the Air Service.

In 1935, Foulois, now a major general, retired. It was to be another twelve years before the modern U.S. Air Force was to become a reality and thirty-four years before military aviation would put a man on the moon. In 1966, he suffered a stroke and died April 25, 1967, in Washington.

Foulois, however, never forgot that Texas was the place which had given him the opportunity to prove his belief that the airplane could become one of the most effective weapons in the arsenal of the military. Even when he was in his eighties, he often returned to Fort Sam Houston for visits and was a popular speaker at service clubs throughout the state.

Benjamin Delahauf Foulois was a Connecticut Yankee and he remained a New Englander until the end. But he always considered Texas his "home away from home," because it was here that his experiments gave impetus to the development of aviation around the world.

And it was in Texas, three miles as the bird flies from the Alamo, that Foulois launched this nation's domination of the air.

Texans almost hanged Edmund Jackson Davis once before he became the Governor. Once he was in the office, he refused to give it up without a fight.

—From portrait in State Capitol, Austin

154

The Governor Who Wouldn't Quit

In most cases, when a new Governor of Texas assumes the office, the transition is tranquil and there are smiles and an exchange of handshakes between the outgoing occupant and the new one. That was not the case, however, when the first Republican to be elected governor refused to vacate the office when he was defeated. Instead of leaving gracefully, he turned the Capitol into an armed fortress protected by his secret police.

He was Edmund J. Davis, perhaps the most feared and certainly the most hated chief executive in the state's history. Remembered as a petty tyrant and a virtual dictator during the four years he held the office, history records that he also was the first and only governor to barely escape hanging by his future constituents. Yet ironically Davis's body rests today in a grave marked by the tallest monument in the State Cemetery in Austin.

Who was this enigma of a man who is remembered on the one hand as a brilliant jurist and an excellent Army field general and yet is called the "scalawag governor" by history? What was the driving ambition that made him try to hold onto an office from which the electorate had removed him and who even demanded that the President of the United States send the Army to assure him another term as governor of Texas?

He was, by all accounts, a complicated personality. A Florida native, he had come to Texas in 1838 with his widowed

155

mother when he was only eleven. Settling in Galveston, he had studied law in Corpus Christi and later practiced there and in Laredo and Brownsville. Regarded by those who knew him well as a man of integrity, culture and impeccable social conduct, he seemed to have a promising career in politics. In 1861, he was a district judge in Brownsville and there was talk that he would be governor one day.

There was talk in Texas, however, of secession from the Union and possible Civil War. Davis shared these Southern sentiments and when Texas called a convention to consider leaving the United States, he was a candidate for the office of delegate. He was defeated, however, and the loss not only embittered him but likely was the factor that changed his life. He became an active Unionist, escaped to Mexico and when the war began, organized a regiment of Texans to fight against the Confederacy.

Davis's First Texas Cavalry was the first, and by far the most important, unit of troops from this state to fight under the Stars and Stripes. He gathered them together in New Orleans, but on December 31, 1862, left there for Galveston where he hoped to pick up more recruits. They arrived January 2, but Galveston had fallen back into the hands of the Confederacy and Davis and his troops barely escaped capture.

Although he escaped the Confederates at Galveston, Davis was destined not to escape later in Mexico. After bringing his Texas Cavalry to the Rio Grande, Davis left his troops aboard ship and went into Matamoros on March 6, 1863. The Confederates at Brownsville were ready for a Federal invasion, but did not expect one. They felt that Davis had stopped only to pick up his family in Mexico and then would return to New Orleans.

Not all of the Confederates accepted this theory, however, and on March 15, a group styling themselves the "Texas Rangers" crossed the river without orders and captured Davis and four others. They carried them back to Texas, hanged one of the men and planned to execute Davis. Mexico was a neutral country, though, and when the governor of the state of Tamaulipas insisted that the capture of Davis was a violation of the laws of neutrality, the Texans reluctantly released him.

Thus saved from certain death at the hands of the Texans, Davis returned with his troops to New Orleans and engaged the Confederates in a skirmish on the Amite River. In the fall of 1863, Davis and the First Texas were ordered back to Galveston in an attempt to take Beaumont and the railroad connecting that place with Houston. That campaign also failed and again the First Texas went back to New Orleans.

West of New Orleans, Davis and his cavalry were involved in a fight at Vermillion Bayou — one of the few battles in which two units made up of Texans would fight as enemies during the Civil War. After this affair, Davis and his troops were sent back to Texas again, this time to take part in the Rio Grande Campaign. The First Texas was part of a force of some 7,000 men whose objective was to take control of the river and they did succeed in capturing Ringgold Barracks at Rio Grande City. Later Davis was placed in command of all Federal cavalry troops in Texas and promoted to brigadier general.

By December, 1864, the cause of the Confederacy appeared lost. General Robert E. Lee was in retreat in Virginia and the Union seemed to be winning on all fronts. General Davis was sent to Galveston to negotiate surrender there, and on June 5, 1865, the flag of the United States was raised over that key Gulf port. Davis and his First Texas Cavalry were mustered out the following November and the commander returned to Texas to resume his political career. General Phil Sheridan, the commander of the military government, offered to appoint Davis chief justice of the Texas Supreme Court but he refused.

The ex-Secessionist who had become a turncoat because he had lost an election now wanted to prove that he could win an elective office. He was named a delegate to the Constitutional Convention of 1866 and was president of the Convention of 1868-1869. He advocated the disfranchisement of all Confederates, unrestricted votes for Negroes and a number of other measures regarded as radical by most Texans. He also tried to divide Texas into three states.

He failed to divide the state geographically, but did succeed in getting nominated in 1869 to run for governor against Andrew Jackson Hamilton, another former officer in the Union Army. Davis had the support of the military in the race and the outspoken support of the new president of the United States, General Ulysses S. Grant. He won the election by a few more than 800 votes, then proceeded to give Texas a gubernatorial administration unlike any in its history.

For four years, Davis was an avowed dictator, appointing more than 8,000 to key positions and demanding their unquestioned loyalty. He also created a force of secret police, and when his tyrannical policies caused riots, he used his troops to enforce martial law. The "Carpetbag Constitution" forced on Texas by the Union gave Governor Davis almost unlimited powers and he used them to impose his rule in every area of government.

By 1873, when the next elections came, Texans had had enough of Davis's reign of terror. By a majority of more than 40,000 votes, they elected Richard Coke over Davis. Coke was a Virginian who had come to Texas in 1849, began practicing law in Waco, was a captain in the Confederacy and had been elected to the Texas Supreme Court in 1866. He was removed from that position by General Sheridan, however, because he claimed that Coke was "an impediment to Reconstruction."

Despite the large majority by which Coke had been elected to the office of governor, Davis declared the election "unconstitutional" and announced that he would not give up the office. The Supreme Court, occupied entirely by judges sympathetic to the Union and to Davis, upheld his claim.

Despite the court's ruling, the new Legislature met in Austin on January 18, 1874, to organize the government. Davis, as expected, refused to recognize it. He barricaded himself in the basement of the Capitol, ordered his secret police to protect him and refused to give up the ballots that had been cast for all state offices. After a week of negotiations between the Legislature, meeting on the second floor, and the barricaded governor in the basement, the ballots were released. They were counted in a joint session of both houses and Richard Coke was declared the elected governor and R.B. Hubbard the lieutenant governor.

Davis still refused to give up. He telegraphed President Grant asking him to intervene by sending the U. S. Army to Austin to prevent Coke from assuming the office to which he had been duly and honestly elected. Grant, although a strong supporter of Davis, knew that the battle was lost and sent the following telegram to the recalcitrant occupant of the office:

"Would it not be prudent, as well as right, to yield to the verdict of the people as expressed by their ballots?"

Davis still refused to give up the office. However, Coke —

who had been sworn in as governor by the Legislature on January 14 despite the armed camp one floor below — had enlisted Austin's Travis Rifles as his own posse "to keep the peace." Fortunately the secret police and Coke's posse never had an actual confrontation, although there were two or three near misses. Finally on January 17, Davis locked the governor's office and slipped out of the Capitol to the home of a friend. Coke had to break down the door with an axe the next day in order to take his place at the governor's desk.

Thus ended Texas's own miniature version of its own Civil War. Governor Coke served his term, was reelected for another in 1876 and resigned in 1877 to become U. S. Senator from Texas. By then, however, he had restored law and order to Texas, returned their civil rights to the people and started Texas on its way to a new era.

Davis continued to make his home in Austin where he was a successful lawyer and a leader of the Republican Party. In 1880, he made another try for the office he had fought so hard to keep but lost by more than 100,000 votes to Oran M. Roberts. Powerful party leaders tried unsuccessfully to get President Chester A. Arthur to name Davis to his cabinet, but he refused. In 1882, Davis ran for Congress and again was defeated. He died the following year.

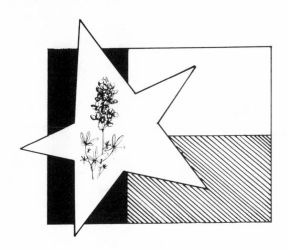

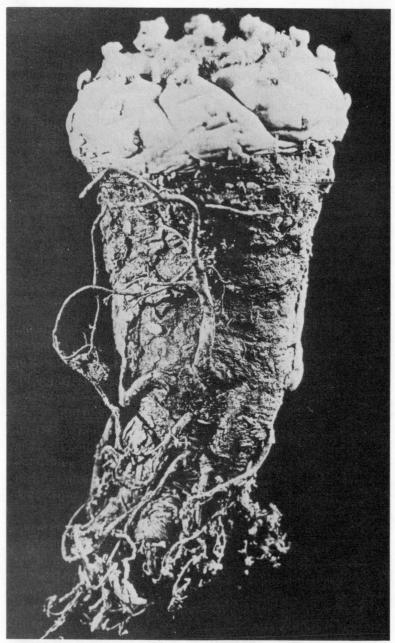

Most Texans have never seen peyote, a plant that looks like a carrot but is a potent hallucinogen. It's illegal to grow or use except in Mirando City, Texas.

—Photo from San Antonio *Express-News*

The Texas Town
Where Drugs Are Legal

They come from places like Little Water, New Mexico, Chicken Bite, Arizona, Colony, Oklahoma, and equally little known towns in Nevada, California, Colorado, Missouri and other states. Their destination is a dying, dusty, one-time boom town in the Texas desert thirty-four miles east of Laredo on the Mexican border. It's name is Mirando City and it is to members of the Native American Church what Mecca is to Moslems.

In mid-February, usually around the 19th and following, Mirando City's population (720) will be increased half again by pilgrims from this unusual Christian Cult. The reason? The Texas border town is the only source of supply of a little-known hallucinogen known as peyote — a drug that is illegal to possess by anybody except Indians who are members of this particular church. For those who are at least one-quarter Indian and who are bona fide members of the Native American Church, use of the drug as a religious sacrament is blessed by both the U.S. and Texas governments.

So each February, leaders of the 350,000-plus members of the church gather in Mirando City at the height of the peyote harvest season. These elders, known as "road men" in the parlance of the denomination, come not only to spend a day or two or three in sending up prayers to God in huge puffs of peyote smoke. They come also to stock up on the drug to take back to their communicants who, because of distance or financial hardship, can't make the trip to what the Indians regard as a holy city.

161

Mirando City and its neighbor, Oilton, are regarded as such because they are the only source of supply, illegal or otherwise, of peyote. It is one of the rarest of the hallucinogens. The only place that this unique cactus plant grows outside of Mexico are the four Texas counties of Webb, Zapata, Starr and Jim Hogg. Here the small, carrot-like plant (known to science as *Lophophora williamsii*) grows wild. The tops, when dried properly, resemble large buttons. When eaten or brewed into a tea, they produce remarkable visions, dreams and hallucinations.

To the Indians, however, peyote is not a drug but a sacrament that is as important to their religious observance as bread and wine are to other Christians. For centuries before the Spanish conquistadors invaded Mexico, the tribes gathered along the Rio Grande for ancient rites featuring the cactus. The Aztecs called peyote *teonactl*, or "god flesh," and used it not only as a sacrament but as a medicine. Its use over the centuries finally persuaded both the Federal and Texas governments to approve the use of the drug under controlled conditions and limiting such use to practicing members of the Native American sect.

It was not until 1968, however, that Texas agreed with U.S. authorities that peyote could be used as an adjunct to religious services. Until then, Texas had had a strict law against such use. However, that law was declared unconstitutional by then District Judge E. James Kazen who wrote in his opinion:

"The evidence . . . has shown that peyotism is a recognized, bona fide religion practiced by members of the New American Church, and that peyote is an essential ingredient of the religious ceremony; It is the sole means by which members of the church are able to experience their religion, and without peyote, the court finds from the evidence, the members of the religion cannot practice their faith."

This landmark decision not only won Judge Kazen honorary membership in the Native American Church, but also gives him the right to attend the ceremonies each year in Mirando City. He is one of the few non-Indians ever allowed to attend these rites.

These ceremonies apparently have changed little over the centuries. They were practiced in Mexico for hundreds of years before they were revived in the U.S. in the 1880s by the Kiowas and the Comanches as a Christian cult. Before Federal controls were placed on peyote as an hallucinogen, the cactus buttons were shipped to Indians throughout the country by the post office at Mirando City. It is still shipped today, but only to designated leaders of units of the Native American Church. One of the reasons for the annual gathering in Mirando City by these leaders is the opportunity the rites afford for them to pick up enough peyote to supply their congregations at home.

The Texas rituals are held in a huge teepee, or lodge, made from twenty-four poles cut from spruce and brought to Mirando City years ago from Utah by the Ute Indians. The poles, each twenty-five feet in length, are wrapped in canvas, completely closing the teepee except for a smoke hole at the top. To accommodate those attending, two such lodges usually are constructed.

Inside the structure, a horseshoe shaped mound of earth is built as an altar. This represents the incomplete life of Jesus Christ which will not be completed until his return to Earth. Inside the altar, a fire is built using logs from a red elm tree that is still alive and standing. In the teepee in which the Comanches worship, the fire can be built of wood from another tree.

During the actual ceremony, which begins at sunset and goes beyond sunrise, music is provided by drums and rattles. The worshippers sit around the altar. Some may eat the dried peyote buttons which, say non-Indians who have sampled them, smell rank and taste horrible. A jug of brew made from the peyote also is passed around in a communal cup, along with a pipe of tobacco. The Comanches again differ from the other tribes in that they prefer to smoke cigarettes wrapped in corn silk.

For the next twelve to sixteen hours, the participants eat or drink peyote, make testimonials, pray, engage in silent contemplation and shake their rattles and beat their drums. The fragrant herb, sage, is used to purify the air in the stifling teepee and often peyote buttons are also thrown on the fire. The Indians who participate in the rites say they do not suffer any effects from the drug — a fact which non-participants in Mirando City say is true.

This is not so, however, for non-communicants of the Native American Church. In the 1950s and 1960s, hippies from around the country heard about the "visions" induced by the peyote button and rushed to the border. They invaded the private ranches where the cactus is grown and dozens of them tried the drug. Almost without exception, it made them violently ill. It also changed the attitude of many ranchers who, under government license and supervision, had grown the cactus to sell to the Indians. Many simply locked their gates and barred their land to everyone.

As a result, the supply of peyote has been slowly diminishing at a time when membership in the Native American Church is increasing. Amade Cardenas until her retirement in 1981, was the "peyote queen of South Texas." She and her husband Claudio went to court in the 1950s and with the help of Indian lawyers, won the right to sell peyote to members of the church. In those days, peyote was so plentiful that the Cardenases sometimes sold the buttons for as little as 75¢ per thousand.

Slowly the price has risen — to $2.50 per thousand, then to $40 per thousand by the mid-1970s. Now the cactus is in such short supply that the latest price is about $80 per 1,000 buttons.

Until the ranchers in the area began closing their properties to avoid the invasion by hippies looking for drugs, the cultivation of peyote provided welcome additional income. Although they had to have a government permit and the crop was always under the watchful eye of U. S. Food and Drug agents, large ranchers could expect to make as much as $1,500 annually off a crop that cost them nothing and which required no care.

At harvest time, dealers (again under government license and supervision) sent cutters onto the land to collect the precious buttons. Both the ranchers and the dealers are required to keep detailed records of their transactions and are allowed to sell only to card-carrying members of the Native American Church. These regulations and controls have not been welcomed by the Indians. They remember that in the 1880s, when the Comanches and Kiowas started the trading in peyote, the ranchland was open to anybody to harvest at any time. Then the Indians had ready access to their sacrament without cost.

Even today, the Indians feel that the peyote belongs to them and they cannot understand the reason for the high prices and the so-called "shortage" of the cactus. They do know that acres of the plant still grow wild throughout the four Texas counties. They say the only shortage is the result of the refusal of ranchers to permit its harvest.

Leaders of the Native American Church find the situation particularly galling since they point out that Indians have used peyote as a religious sacrament for at least 2,000 years. Although many tribes knew and used the drug before the birth of Christ, it continued as a part of their worship after missionaries converted them to Christianity. Some of the tribes have a legend that when Jesus was on the cross and his side was pierced, each drop of blood that fell onto the ground produced a peyote plant. Thus they regard the little spineless cactus as a holy gift without which their religion would lose much of its meaning.

As one leader of the Native American Church told a reporter at the rites in Mirando City:

"Our medicine grows here and we want to worship where it grows. This is our Holy Land, our Jerusalem."

Joseph Heneage Finch, Seventh Earl of Aylesford, lived in Texas only twenty months, but he may have been the biggest spender and hardest drinker ever to try ranching.

—Photo from the San Angelo *Standard-Times*

Of Cow Servants and
Cattle Estates

It has been almost a century now since the last "cow servant" herded cattle on a Texas ranch. And there isn't an old-timer alive who remembers when the "proprietors" — they disliked being called "ranchers" — rode their range sitting on hornless saddles astride blooded horses. Instead of Levis, chaps and the inevitable Stetson, their work clothing was most often gray corduroy knickers, English riding boots and a red hunting cap.

They belonged to an era long past, these titled noblemen from Great Britain. But between 1880 and 1900, wealthy with profits made during the economic imperialism of the Victorian period, they headed for Texas. Their goal was to make money, but they were looking for excitement, too. They hoped to find both by buying "cattle estates" somewhere south of the Red River and west of the Pecos.

One of the first to come was Sir Dudley Coutts Marjoribanks (pronounced "Marshbanks"), the first Baron of Tweedsmouth. In 1883, he headed a syndicate that bought 244 square miles that spread over Collingsworth and Wheeler Counties. Here, in the southern Panhandle of Texas, he established Rocking Chair Ranche, Limited, popularly known to his neighbors as "Nobility Ranch" because the owners were all titled British aristocracy.

Over the next two decades, others were to follow Lord Tweedsmouth's example. The interest of the British super-rich was so intense, in fact, that Francis Smith, a New York stockbroker, headed for Texas and set himself up as a land agent. Operating out of San Antonio, and with branch offices in Houston and Fort Worth, he developed a profitable business enticing the English, Scotch and Irish into converting their British pounds into Texas real estate.

Whether Joseph Heneage Finch, the seventh Earl of Aylesford, was a client of Smith's or not, he was destined to become the most memorable Englishman to adopt Texas as home. He also was the biggest spender, the hardest drinker and the shortest lived — his residence in and about the frontier town of Big Spring totaled only twenty months.

In England, the Earl — "Sporting Joe," his friends called him — had moved in the right circles. He was something of an athlete and a whiz at polo. One of his close friends was the Prince of Wales, later to be King Edward VII of the British Empire. It was while on a hunting trip with the Prince to India in 1876 that the Earl made his decision to forsake England forever and find a home in Texas.

A marital problem started it all. While hunting with the future King, he received a letter from his wife. She wanted a divorce so she could marry Lord Blandford, a future Duke of Marlborough and the uncle of Winston Churchill. She was, she wrote, pregnant by Blandford.

The Earl of Aylesford, as always, was a good sport about it all and gave her the divorce. He didn't even follow the tradition of English gentlemen and call Blandford out for a duel, probably because the Prince of Wales talked him out of it. However, he did decide to leave England forever and he chose to move to Texas. In August, 1883, he arrived in Big Spring.

His arrival in the West Texas town was an occasion. Legend says that Jay Gould, the railroad builder, personally brought him there aboard his luxurious private railroad car. It is more likely, however, that one of Gould's staff was the escort. At any rate, he was met at the station by John Birdwell, the proprietor of a Big Spring saloon and a kind of unofficial greeter of visiting celebrities. When "Sporting Joe" was introduced as the Seventh Earl of Aylesford, Birdwell — a one-time Texas Ranger — was dumbfounded.

"Anybody with a handle like that would be shot out here," Birdwell told him. "From now on, you're simply 'Judge' Finch." And so he was.

Since it was late afternoon and no provision had been made to transport the titled Britisher and his considerable entourage of servants to the four-section ranch he had bought sight unseen thirteen miles out of Big Spring, he was escorted to the Cosmopolitan Hotel. The clapboard building lacked the amenities of even the smallest English country inns, but it was the only hostel in town. Unfortunately it had no vacancies and none of the guests was willing to give up his room, even to a foreign nobleman.

Unruffled by this lack of hospitality from his new neighbors, the Earl solved the problem on the spot. He simply called for the owner, bought the hotel and ousted enough of the paying guests so that he and his aides could move in. The price? $1,000 in British pound sterling. Legend has it that he gave the hotel back to its owner the next day with the restriction that he was to have a room anytime he wanted it. Although he planned to live on his ranch, he expected to visit "the city" at every opportunity.

Once settled, the Earl outfitted himself in spurs, Texas boots and the other accepted regalia of the range. The cowboys in the area, however, remained suspicious of this tenderfoot with the funny accent and refused to accept his company. This concerned the newcomer and he decided to do something about it at the spring roundup in 1884 when cow punchers from all of the ranches in the area gathered to bring in all of the strays.

The Earl brought along a ten-gallon keg of whiskey and invited all of the men to drink their fill. They did. In fact, the hands got so drunk that they couldn't complete the roundup. The occasion endeared the Earl to them, but not their bosses. His fellow ranchers were cool to him for weeks.

This the Seventh Earl of Aylesford found difficult to understand, for drinking to him was as necessary — perhaps more so — as eating. It was said that he drank a half gallon of whiskey every day and sometimes chased it with two or three bottles of gin. One visitor to his ranch said that the pile of empty liquor bottles in the side yard was higher than the ranch house.

Along with strong drink, the Earl loved good food. Like most Englishmen, he favored mutton and lamb — meats that were scarce at that time in an area where beef was considered the only edible meat. When he discovered that the town's only butcher shop couldn't supply him, he built his own — a stone edifice which today is the oldest structure in Big Spring.

Although he was addicted to both strong drink and good food, he remained aloof from women during his almost two years in Big Spring. Handsome, debonair and rich, he was regarded as a "good catch" by the local girls. He limited his social life primarily to drinking with neighbors and to hunting. Having hunted most of the world for big game, he spent as much time as possible stalking the deer and antelope prevalent in the area.

His hunting trips were the talk of West Texas. He always took along a retinue of servants. His equipment included not only the finest guns, but tents and even furniture. He insisted on camping always near a running stream where a servant prepared his bath each morning. Even in freezing weather, the Earl insisted on his morning wash.

Although his income from the family estates in England was more than $50,000 a year — incredible wealth in a Texas town where $30 a month was considered a living wage — the Earl managed it poorly. While he had brought with him an Anglican bishop to serve as both his spiritual and financial advisor, the Earl was his own man when it came to spending money.

Unhappy because the Big Spring saloons didn't stock the Scotch whisky and gins that suited his tastes, he bought his own watering place. He instructed the bartender to lay in only the best and the drinks were always "on the house" to his friends and the cowboys from the outlying ranches.

He bought cattle with the same abandon that he did whiskey. To stock his new ranch, he paid $40,000 for a herd of cattle without even seeing the cows. As a residence for himself and staff, he built an eleven-room story-and-a-half ranch house, a huge barn and outbuildings. He set aside two acres for kennels to house the dozens of hunting dogs he brought with him from England. In keeping with the tradition of wealthy Englishmen, he also brought over his private carriage and liveried coachman.

Within a year, it was apparent to his neighbors that the Earl's money was running out. From England came word that his mother, the Dowager Countess Lady Aylesford, had cut his annual income from the family. The Earl rushed back to London to try and start the cash flow again but apparently was unsuccessful. He sold his own properties there, borrowed money from a brother and returned to Texas.

However, his health was failing, too. He had been seeing a Big Spring doctor regularly before he went back to England. While there he had become involved in a fight at a railway station and broke his leg. This injury was still troubling him when he returned to Texas but his illness was more serious than just a broken bone that was slow to heal.

It was nearing Christmas, 1884, when the Earl returned to Big Spring and he decided to celebrate the holiday with the biggest party he had ever hosted. It was, of course, at the Cosmopolitan Hotel and the saloon he owned and the butcher shop he had built supplied the food and drink. It lasted two weeks and most of the ranchers and cowboys in the area attended all, or part, of it.

Long before it ended, however, the Earl took to his bed. By January 6, 1885, he was so ill that the doctor remained constantly at his bedside. Then on the morning of the 13th, he got up, dressed and ate a huge meal with his friends. With a half gallon of Scotch at his side, he began a game of euchre with some of his guests. Even drunk he was a brilliant card player and he seemed to be enjoying the game immensely.

After awhile, however, he excused himself, said, "So long, boys," went to his bedroom and died. He was thirty-six years old.

The next day, *The Pantagraphic*, the Big Spring weekly paper, announced his passing to the world. "The Judge is Dead!" the headline on page one read.

Years later, the citizens of Big Spring honored that most unique pioneer by naming a street after him. By then, however, memory had dimmed and the street — which still serves the community was misspelled "Aylford."

The Non-Union Man

When Texas voted on whether or not it should become one of the United States of America in 1845, the decision was not unanimous. A husband-wife spat caused one of the delegates to cast a negative vote.

The "nay" vote is the only one recorded in the Convention of 1845, called by the Republic of Texas to decide the statehood issue. It was cast by Richard Bache, a grandson of Benjamin Franklin and brother-in-law to George M. Dallas, then vice president of the country Texas was about to join.

It was the fact that Bache's wife was the sister of the U. S. vice president that prompted his opposition to annexation. Nine years earlier, for reasons lost to history, Bache had deserted his wife and the nine children she had borne him and headed for Texas. Apparently his dislike for his ex-spouse extended to her family. Although Bache personally favored statehood for Texas, he voted "no" because he wanted no part of a Union in which his wife's brother held the Number Two job in the government.

If Bache's vote surprised his fellow delegates, the fact that he was there at all must have been a cause for wonderment. Despite his illustrious heritage, Bache apparently had not inherited any of his famous grandfather's talents or charisma. Until his election by the citizens of Galveston to represent them at the convention on statehood, he was known in the community mainly as a hard drinker who had a difficult time getting and keeping a job.

Bache was born in Philadelphia in 1784, the son of a wealthy merchant and Benjamin Franklin's attractive daughter, Sarah. At the age of twenty-one, he married a beautiful socialite, Sophia B. Dallas, whose father was serving in President Madison's cabinet as treasury secretary. It appeared to be the perfect union and Philadelphians confidently predicted that the young couple would one day be the lions of local society.

And so it appeared to be — at first. When the War of 1812 began, Bache, as any scion of a wealthy family was expected to do, marched off with Franklin's Flying Artillery, serving as captain of the Philadelphia Volunteers. When the war ended, President Madison promptly rewarded him by appointing him postmaster of Philadelphia. Thus he took the first step toward what many believed was a road to high political office.

Unfortunately, however, Bache didn't give as much attention to the job as he might have. Indeed he somehow failed to report all of his sales of postage stamps to Washington. If these discrepancies in the accounts were reported to President Madison, he chose to ignore them. His successor, James Monroe, also took no action about the Philadelphia post office problem. But in 1828, President John Quincy Adams decided the bad bookkeeping had gone on long enough. He personally removed Bache from the postmaster's job, announcing that shortages in the official accounts exceeded $25,000.

What happened during the next eight years is somewhat lost to history. It is known that the government made some effort to collect the losses of the Philadelphia post office from Bache but without success. Apparently his wife's family supported the Baches and their growing brood and this dependence may have been the root of their marital problems. At any rate, in 1836 Bache walked out on Sophia and the children.

Later that year, he showed up in Texas as a private in the Independent Volunteers, a company neighboring Louisiana had sent over to help in the war of independence against Mexico. If Bache distinguished himself as a soldier, it doesn't show up in the records. After the Battle of San Jacinto, he was one of the enlisted men assigned to guard the captured Mexican dictator, Santa Anna.

Even that duty, however, brought only criticism of his liking for alcohol. Colonel Gabriel Nunez Ortego, an aide to Santa Anna, wrote in 1836 that one of the worst things about the general's imprisonment at Velasco was "being bored by the drunken grandson of Benjamin Franklin." Shortly after, Bache was out of the Texian Army and, at age forty-two, broke and jobless.

Like many another veteran before and since, Bache worked at anything he could get, often "moonlighting" on two, and sometimes three, jobs at once. His wife, despite her own wealth, kept demanding some support for herself and the nine offspring back in Philadelphia. Bache needed every dollar he could earn.

In December, 1837, his status as a veteran of the revolution helped to get him hired as a Navy Department clerk in Houston. Two days later, when the secretary of the navy left his post, Bache was asked to serve as secretary since there was no one else available in the small department of the struggling Republic. A week later, the position had been filled and Bache was back at his clerk's desk. On June 4, 1838, he was promoted to chief clerk. Apparently that job didn't pay enough, however, and by September he was carried on the navy payroll twice — both as chief clerk and as clerk. On the side he was working as enrolling clerk in the House of Representatives in the capitol in Houston.

In 1842, Bache moved to Galveston where he continued as a navy clerk. After only a few weeks, however, he was named commander of the Navy Yard there and this position gave him a new status in the community which he had not enjoyed since he left Philadelphia.

In Washington meanwhile, President James K. Polk had pushed the annexation of Texas as one of the major goals of his administration. To garner support for the proposal, he sent his vice president, George M. Dallas, on a speech-making crusade. Bache, who favored statehood for Texas but despised the idea of having his brother-in-law next in line for the U. S. presidency, said little but thought a lot. He became a candidate for election as a delegate to the convention to decide whether or not Texas should join the Union.

Getting elected probably was no easy task for Bache. His liking for saloons and the products they vended had not diminished with his rise to Navy Yard commander. He was often seen drunk on the streets of Galveston.

The voters chose to ignore this weakness in Bache's character and duly elected him as their delegate. Thus provided with a platform from which he could publicly express his bitterness toward his wife and the high office her brother held in the U. S. government, Bache cast the only dissenting vote against Texas's becoming one of the United States.

Fortunately the majority ruled and Texas went on to join the Union while Bache returned to Galveston. The citizens there, seemingly understanding the unique domestic squabble that had caused their representative to oppose statehood, reacted by selecting him to help draw up the new state's first Constitution. Then they proceeded to elect him as senator to represent them in the Second Texas Legislature.

Back in Philadelphia, Bache had become something of the forgotten man. The Federal government, failing in its efforts to collect from him any of the $25,000 in postal funds that he was suspected of misappropriating, filed a suit against his mother's estate. In May, 1833, the government won its case and collected $22,235, much of it representing the inheritance that Sarah Franklin Bache had received from her famous father.

Apparently Sophia Bache and the children had fared well without him, too. Since she had been born to both wealth and social position, Mrs. Bache saw to it that her family had the best of everything. One son, Alexander Dallas Bache, finished first in his class at the U. S. Military Academy and had established himself as a distinguished scientist by the time his father was serving in the Senate of Texas.

And what of Senator Bache? On March 17, 1848, he fell dead on an Austin street and probably was buried in Oakwood Cemetery there. However, his grave is not marked and cemetery records do not show the burial of a Richard Bache.

There are those who believe that Bache's death may have been brought on by a stroke of apoplexy caused when he learned that a settler named John Neely Bryan had started a new community on the Trinity River in North Texas. Bryan called his settlement "Dallas."

Bache's death incidentally, came while his despised brother-in-law still held office. Vice President Dallas didn't end his term until almost a year later.

Was the late David Guion of Dallas the composer of the official song of Kansas? It's a question that Kansans feel has never been properly answered.

Home On The Range:
The Off-Key Story of a Song

If a new Civil War ever erupts again in these United States, it may be between Kansas and Texas. At issue will be which state gave the ballad, *Home on the Range*, to the world of music.

Although *Home on the Range* may not be in the repertoire of most rock groups, it is still one of the all-time hit tunes about the American West. It was, so Kansas sources insist, written by a homesteader in the Sunflower State more than a century ago. It did not surface on the national music scene until the 1920s. In the 1930s, it was the favorite song of President Franklin D. Roosevelt. And just about every vocalist who was anybody in the Thirties and Forties recorded it at least once.

In Kansas, *Home on the Range* is sung with the same kind of reverence with which The University of Texas alumni render *The Eyes of Texas*. Maybe even more so because, unlike "The Eyes" which is just a college alma mater, "Home" is the official hymn of the state of Kansas. It has been since 1947, and Kansas wants the world to know that it was written by a Kansan.

The problem is that a Texan is accepted by most authorities as the composer of *Home on the Range*. His name was David W. Guion and he lived in Dallas until his death. He said that he wrote the song when he was a lad of fifteen. And he did hold the copyright and he collected the royalties all of those years.

Not only that, but Mr. Guion was a composer whose works

have won international acclaim. He produced more than 200 original compositions, plus many orchestral and piano transcriptions of old fiddle tunes that are known to fanciers of country western music as "hoedowns." His symphony, *Texas Suite*, received the plaudits of the critics. His Broadway musicals were hits. In fact, his credentials as a composer are impeccable.

So what's all the hassle about who composed *Home on the Range*?

There is no doubt that the first version of what we know as the song's lyrics date back nineteen years before David Guion was born. One day in 1873, a physician named Brewster Higley who had homesteaded in Smith County, Kansas, picked up a piece of foolscap and wrote a poem about his "home where the buffalo roam." It was published shortly after in the local newspaper, the Smith County *Pioneer*, under the title that Dr. Higley gave it, "Western Home."

The doctor intended it only as a poetic tribute to his new, adopted homeland on the prairie. However, a neighbor named Dan Kelly, who played guitar in a frontier orchestra, read the words to "Western Home" and set them to music. The ballad was first played and sung not long after at a country dance near Harlan, Kansas.

Sometime later either Dr. Higley or Kelly — historians have not been able to verify which one — moved south to the Texas Panhandle as commercial buffalo hunters followed the herds there. The song, "Western Home," was popular with the hunters and was sung most nights around campfires throughout the range country. The words changed somewhat as the song was passed along by impromptu singers and it became generally known under the title "On the Buffalo Range." When the great Texas buffalo hunt ended in 1877, the song was picked up by cowboys driving cattle herds up the trail to Kansas.

By 1890, when most of the trail drives had ended, "On the Buffalo Range" was being sung by cowboys in at least three states — Texas, Oklahoma and Kansas. Certainly the song was well-known when David Wendell de Fentresse Guion was born on December 15, 1892. His birthplace was his family's T-O-Bar-G Ranch ten miles west of Ballinger in Runnels County. His father, John I. Guion, a descendant of an old French family, was a prominent rancher and lawyer. His mother, the former Matilda Armour de Fentresse, also claimed a long French ancestry. Mrs. Guion was a gifted pianist and singer, and from the time David was born, both parents pointed him toward a career in music.

He did not disappoint them. He was playing the piano almost by the time he could talk. He wrote his first musical composition when he was four. By the time he was old enough to be shipped off to Whipple Academy in Illinois, he already was an accomplished pianist and composer. Later he continued his musical education at Fort Worth's Polytechnic College, then went to Vienna for three years at the Royal Conservatory of Music.

In 1907, when fifteen-year-old David was home from school for summer vacation, he wrote down the words to a song he had first heard the cowboys on the ranch sing a couple of years before. The song was "On the Buffalo Range." David changed the title and some of the words to suit himself as he wrote them down. To the young composer, the song was pure folk poetry and he wanted to preserve it, but he didn't like the tune to which it was sung. He adapted it to a more graceful melody of his composition — the tune by which we know the song today.

The next year, John A. Lomax, The University of Texas folklorist, was putting together a collection of cowboy songs. The great Negro folksinger, Leadbelly, had given Lomax a song called *Home on the Range*. In 1910, when Lomax published his collection, he included the song, but did not credit it to any composer.

Detractors of Guion's claim to the composition say the publication of *Home on the Range* in the Lomax collection proves that the song had been around for years. Guion said that this wasn't true. He contended that, in the three years between the time he wrote his version and the time Lomax picked it up from Leadbelly, the new words and tune had been sung around the state. He believed that a Negro servant at the Guion ranch passed the song on to Leadbelly.

Nothing much was heard of *Home on the Range* until the late 1920s. Guion was asked to stage a cowboy revue at the old Roxy Theater in New York. For the revue, he resurrected the version of *Home on the Range* that he had written as a youngster. It became an overnight hit.

179

One who especially liked the song was Franklin D. Roosevelt. When he was sworn in as president of the United States on March 4, 1932, *Home on the Range* became a kind of unofficial presidential song. It was played wherever Roosevelt appeared in public during his more than twelve years in the White House. Perhaps the government of the People's Republic of China got the idea in the Roosevelt era that *Home on the Range* was equal to *Hail to the Chief* as a way to welcome a United States President. In 1972, when Richard Nixon visited China, the band struck up "Home" as he dined with Chinese leaders in the Great Hall of Peking.

Until *Home on the Range* became a hit in the 1930s, noboby cared much who the composer was. Once the royalties began coming in, however, it was a different story. In 1934, an Arizona couple filed a Federal court suit claiming that they owned the copyright to "My Arizona Home" and that *Home on the Range* was a pirated version of that song. The Music Publishers Protective Association defended the suit.

Its attorney, Samuel Moanfeldt of New York, spent months traveling through the Southwest interviewing former buffalo hunters, trail hands and musicians. In Smith County, Kansas, he located one L. T. Reese who swore that he was one of four persons present when Dr. Higley publicly read his poem for the first time. He also found a man who had been present when Dan Kelly's musical version was first sung.

With these and other witnesses to prove his case, Moanfeldt had only to present his evidence to the court. The judge ruled that "Home on the Range" (at least, the original version) had been written by Dr. Higley and nobody else.

David Guion, of course, has never claimed that he did anything more than revise the original lyrics of the ballad, or the lyrics as he heard them sung by cowboys in 1905. He believes the words probably were sung to the tune which Dan Kelly had put them to when he had first read Dr. Higley's poem. No manuscript of Kelly's melody has ever been found, but Guion recalled that it was "bouncier" than the one he said he wrote for the song in 1907.

Thus there really shouldn't be any controversy over the origins of *Home on the Range*. There is no doubt that the poem did originate in Kansas and was the work of Dr. Brewster Higley. There also is no doubt that the version sung today is much changed from Dr. Higley's original. Certainly nobody questions that the music (at least, the tune by which *Home on the Range* has been sung for more than fifty years) is the authentic work of a distinguished Texas composer, David Guion. And on one point there is no argument: It was Guion, a Texan, who made *Home on the Range* known around the world.

The questions which have never been answered by Kansas detractors of Guion are these: Why did it take the state of Kansas more than sixty years to discover that a ballad called my "Western Home" was written by a Kansan and why did it take even longer for Kansas to get around to adopting it as the state song?

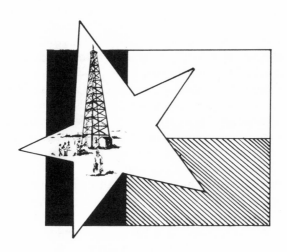

Spy in Petticoats

There's a tiny cemetery at 2911 Washington Street in the shadow of Houston's skyline which holds the bones of one of the most remarkable women in history.

Most Texans have never heard of her and her name is almost never mentioned in history books. Even the simple inscription on her grave — "Mrs. Emma M. Seelye, Army Nurse" — means nothing to the passerby who doesn't know her unusual story. For Emma Seelye was not only a nurse, but one of the most able spies of the Civil War.

Women spies are hardly unique to world history. From *Bible* times to Mata Hari to the use of lady secret agents by the Central Intelligence Agency today, the wiles of the weaker sex always have been useful in extracting secrets from a nation's enemies. Emma Seelye, however, is not even listed in military records and for good reason. She served her entire hitch in the U. S. Army as Private Frank Thompson, a man who could hold his own with any other soldier who wore the blue of the Grand Army of the Republic.

Emma Seelye was born Sarah Emma Evelyn Edmonson in December, 1841, in New Brunswick, Canada, and her strange career as the only woman ever recognized as a spy by the Federal Army began because of a spat with her father. The elder Edmonson had always wanted a son and demanded that his daughter learn to shoot and to ride the fastest horses. Emma tried to be everything her father wanted but recalled that she never remembered a kind word from him. When she was seventeen, he insisted that she marry a neighboring farmer who was much older than she and Emma decided it was time to rebel.

She left home, moved to the United States, changed her name from Emma Edmonson to Frank Thompson and clipped off her brown curls. She settled in Flint, Michigan, and took a job selling books from door-to-door. Then, on May 17, 1861, she decided to respond to the Union's call for volunteers and enlisted under the name of Frank Thompson as a male nurse in the army.

It wasn't difficult. In those troubled times there was no physical examination for enlisted personnel and nobody bothered to scrutinize volunteers very closely. "Private Thompson" could handle a gun with the best of them and knew the rudiments of taking care of the sick and wounded. So far as Company F of the Army of the Potomac was concerned, the new recruit was a good soldier.

Emma Seelye, as Frank Thompson, marched with the Union Army to Manassas, excited with the possibility of meeting the Rebels in battle. Later, however, she was to write that war held no romance for her. "There was suffering of which no pen can ever describe," she said.

Apparently the Army brass decided that Frank Thompson's talents lay outside the field of nursing. At any rate, a regimental order was issued appointing Private Thompson as the company mail carrier. Later Frank became the postmaster for the entire brigade. Not long after, the private was summoned to Washington to be given a test for the U. S. Secret Service. No less a personage than General George B. McClellan was a member of the review board that pronounced Private Thompson fit for assignment as a Union spy.

Emma Seelye had exactly the talents the Union Army wanted in its intelligence operatives. She could outshoot and ride better than most soldiers. She also had the ability to keep a secret, although the Army was unaware that this included her sex.

Her first assignment as "Private Frank Thompson, spy" was to slip behind enemy lines posing as a Negro cook. Apparently Emma was a good makeup artist, too, because she had no trouble carrying out the assignment. She not only noted the fortifications of the Gray Army, but where their guns were placed. She returned with a list of planned troop movements and most of the attack plans of General Robert E. Lee and his Army of the South.

As "Private Thompson," Emma had been so successful as a spy that she was sent on another mission. This time, however, the assignment was easy. The beardless "Thompson" dressed as a woman and invaded the Rebel lines to sell cakes and pies to the soldiers. Again she returned with a superb intelligence report that won the plaudits of her superiors.

However, the strain of being a woman living as a man among an all-male army, plus the rigorous and dangerous assignments she had been given, broke her health. She contracted malaria and had to be hospitalized. Fearful that her sex would be discovered, she asked for a furlough. When it was denied, she deserted and had a nervous breakdown. In 1863, the Army formally listed Private Thompson as a deserter and ordered "his" arrest.

As "Frank Thompson," Emma drifted to Ohio, took a room in a boarding house and stayed long enough to recover from the bout with malaria and the nervous breakdown. Then Thompson, his health apparently regained, left. A few days later, Emma Edmonds (having shortened her maiden name) showed up and rented the same room. There she decided to tell her story to the world by writing a novel which she titled "Nurse and Spy." She was only twenty-three.

The book was a best-seller even by today's standards. More than 175,000 copies were sold and the case of "Private Frank Thompson, woman spy" became a *cause celebre* in Washington Army circles. The top brass denied that it could have happened at all.

Meanwhile, Emma met a man named Linus Seelye and married him. They moved to Saint Mary's Parish, Louisiana, where a daughter and two sons were born to them. After the death of the daughter and one of the sons, the Seelyes moved to Missouri and then to Fort Scott, Kansas. It was while living there that Emma decided to try to clear her name as a soldier so that she could apply for a disability pension.

By now a woman approaching fifty, she journeyed back to Flint, Michigan, where she had enlisted. She wanted to look up her old Army buddies and get them to sign affidavits attesting that they had served with her as Frank Thompson. Several of those with whom she had shared a tent in the field were embarrassed when they recognized her but they signed the documents. On July 5, 1884, Congress passed a bill granting Emma Seelye a Federal pension. Two years later, on July 3, 1886, all charges against Frank Thompson as a deserter were dismissed.

Emma Seelye, her name cleared and her pension secure, continued to battle for her health. The malaria she had contracted in the Army continued to recur. In 1893, when the Seelye's remaining son decided to move to Texas from Kansas, the parents decided to follow. They bought a farm near La Porte, across the bay from the San Jacinto Battleground.

As Emma's health worsened, however, the couple sold their farm and moved into La Porte, buying a small house on the town's Main Street. Then, in April, 1897, she received the greatest honor in her life. The General George B. McClellan Post of the Grand Army of the Republic, headquartered at Houston, invited her to become a member. Thus she became the only woman ever to be given membership in an organization of Civil War veterans that had always been reserved for males.

Emma Seelye died in La Porte and was buried there. But on Memorial Day, 1901, her remains were removed and reburied in Houston. Her fellow members of the Grand Army of the Republic wanted her buried close by so that they could attend her grave.

Today the story of Emma Edmonson, the intrepid young woman who masqueraded as a man in order to serve her country, has not been forgotten. In Fort Scott, Kansas, where she spent some of the happiest years of her life, the Sarah E. Seelye Tent Number 25 of the Daughters of the Union Veterans bears her name. And in Houston, a few still come to visit the grave with the simple marker: "Mrs. Emma E. Seelye, Army Nurse."

Texas Declaration of Independence

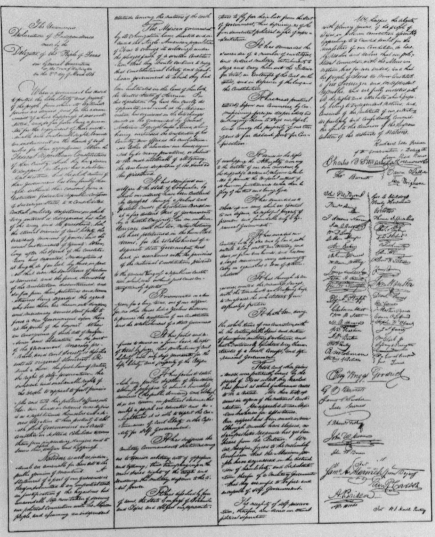

The original Texas Declaration of Independence is eleven pages long, but this traced copy at the Texas Memorial Museum in Austin is the one most familiar to Texans.

—Photo from Archives Division, Texas State Library

Texas Independence Day:
The Holiday That Isn't

It was in a blacksmith shop in a hamlet called Washington that fifty-nine men signed a document declaring that Texas would be forever free of Mexican rule. They dated it March 2, 1836, primarily to boost the ego of one of the signers, an ex-Tennessean named Sam Houston who was celebrating his forty-second birthday. The fact is, however, that the document wasn't signed until the following day — March 3 — and so Texans have been celebrating the wrong holiday since.

That the Texas Declaration bears a date different from the one on which it was signed is but one of the bizarre stories connected with one of the more unique documents in world history. Among other things, the Texas Declaration, unlike the one that freed America from British rule, apparently was the work of one author and not of the Convention assembled. Also unlike the American Declaration of 1776, which had the support of most of the citizenry, many Texans opposed independence from Mexico and some accused the signers of the document of attempting to "steal" Texas. And although the Declaration of Independence one day would become the most sacred document in the archives of a state, it was handled so nonchalantly by its signators that it actually was lost for ninety-three years!

Problems with the Declaration of Independence from Mexico began with the selection of the site where the document was to be drawn. Delegates from various Texas settlements had met in 1835 at San Felipe de Austin, the capital of Stephen F.

George Campbell Childress was a lawyer and newspaper editor in Tennessee who may have written the Declaration of Independence before he ever saw Texas.

— Photo of a portrait from Barker Texas History Center,
University of Texas at Austin

188

Austin's colony, to discuss grievances against Mexico. Accommodations in San Felipe were poor, however, and businessmen in the new town of Washington began a campaign to get future "consultations" moved to their community. The Provisional Government, swayed in its decision by Sam Houston's preference for Washington, reluctantly called for the Convention to meet there March 1, 1836.

The site was not a popular choice. Although Washington already was bragging that it likely would be the future capital of Texas, it was only a hamlet of fewer than one hundred people. It had neither a printing press nor a library. Neither did it have a building large enough to handle a meeting of fifty-nine delegates, plus clerks. Since newspapers were virtually non-existent and the Convention probably wouldn't have been considered newsworthy at the time, there was no need to make provisions for press coverage.

Fortunately, Noah P. Byars, a Washington blacksmith who used his forge mostly to make guns for the expected war with Mexico, was induced by two of the community's boosters to build a larger shop. In turn, they agreed to pay him $170 rental if the place could be turned into a meeting hall for the convention. Byars saw the venture as a profitable way for him to expand his business and agreed.

By March 1, however, Byars had not quite completed the building. It had walls and a roof but no door and the windows had no glass. This might not have been such a hardship if the Spring of 1836 had been mild, but it wasn't. A howling blue norther blew in as the delegates gathered on March 1, forcing them to try to keep warm by putting cloth over the openings in the hall. Many historians believe that the weather was the principal reason the Declaration was written and signed in only three short days of deliberation. The inadequacy of the hall to protect the delegates from the thirty-three-degree temperatures and winds is one explanation as to why Byars was never paid his $170 rental.

Actually three days probably was all of the time the delegates needed to agree to sign the Declaration because there is good reason to believe that it was written before they even met. The likely author was George C. Childress, a thirty-two-year-old lawyer and editor of Tennessee's largest newspaper, the *Nashville Banner and Advertiser*. Wealthy and socially prominent in Tennessee, he became interested in Texas through his uncle, Sterling C. Robertson, who had become a successful impresario here. In November, 1835, Childress, saddened by the death of his wife, left Nashville and headed for Texas.

A moody man given to alternate moments of great elation and deep depression, Childress was convinced that Texas should be independent of Mexico. In Nashville he had made many speeches calling for such freedom and had raised money among rich Tennesseans to support Texas in a war if such became necessary. And in spare moments in his editorial office, he had read and reread the American Declaration of Independence and discussed it as a model for Texas.

Whether he actually arrived in Texas with the draft of such a document in his saddlebags (he made the long trip by horseback) isn't known. What is known is that he was elected a delegate to the Convention and that he called the meeting to order. When he completed the organization of the delegates and appointed a committee to draft a Declaration, he was appointed chairman of that committee. Only hours after he called the committee to work on March 1, word went out that the document was ready and it was presented the next day. Apparently it was approved without debate on the first reading.

However, the first copy apparently had some errors and the delegates put off signing until an engrossed copy could be prepared. This wasn't ready until March 3, when the signatures finally were affixed. March 2 had been spent mostly in celebrating Sam Houston's birthday and that was the date that went on the document.

Then, having voted themselves a Declaration of Independence, the Texans lost it. On the night of the signing, one-hundred copies had been run off so that the various settlements could have one (Childress's signature somehow got left off of these) but the engrossed, official copy was to be sent to Washington for the perusal of the U. S. State Department. Childress and an associate were to be the messengers carrying the document and they were also to urge the American government to send Texas some needed help.

Somehow in the bureaucracy of Washington, D. C., the treasured Declaration from Washington, Texas, disappeared.

Some said that the document never got to Washington at all —
that A.S. Kemble, who was at the Convention but not as a delegate, took it home with him to Kentucky. Some historians
said that it was never lost but was burned years later when the
old Capitol at Austin burned. Finally, in 1896, Seth Sheppard,
a Texan who had become chief justice of the District of Columbia, heard from a friend that the original was still at the U. S.
State Department.

It seems that William H. Wharton, the minister whom
Sam Houston had sent to Washington later in 1836 to represent the Republic of Texas, had left the document with a friend
at State. For sixty years, it had lain forgotten and unnoticed in
a file. Immediately efforts began to get the Declaration back to
Texas.

It finally got to Austin in 1929 and was installed in a special niche on the first floor of the Capitol. It remains there
today, one of the top tourist attractions in the capital city.

Of the fifty-nine who signed the document, only two were
native Texans and both, of course, were Mexicans. One, Jose
Antonio Navarro, was among the twenty-one special commit-
teemen selected by Childress to remain after the signing of the
Declaration to draw up a Constitution for the infant Republic
of Texas. The other native, Jose Francisco Ruiz, spoke no English and had to have the proceedings translated for him.

Among the other signers, five were foreign-born. One each
came originally from England, Scotland, Ireland, Canada and
Mexico. The Mexican was Lorenzo de Zavala, a political refu-
gee from Santa Anna's government, who was a successful land
impresario. De Zavala was destined to become the first vice-
president of the new Republic.

Of the ten United States represented among the signers,
Tennessee and Virginia each furnished eleven. Nine came
from North Carolina, five from Kentucky, and Georgia and
South Carolina each furnished four. There were three from
Pennsylvania, two from New York and one each from Massa-
chusetts and Mississippi.

Unlike many of those who signed the American Declaration of Independence, most of the signers of the Texas document were not men of property or rank. Robert Hamilton, a
Scotch immigrant, was wealthy and George C. Childress was
not poor. Sam Houston already had made a national reputation

as a politician before he left Tennessee for Texas and some, like Collin McKinney, aged seventy, had been around for a long time. For the most part, however, the men who signed the document declaring Texas free and independent of Mexico were ordinary citizens whose role in history was yet to be determined.

McKinney, who would later give his first name to a Texas county and his last name to its principal town, had come to Texas in 1831 and settled on the Arkansas border. He actually thought for many years that he was a resident of Arkansas, not Texas. Even though he later served three terms in the Congress of the Republic of Texas, his status as a citizen remained in question.

Many of those who signed the Declaration all but disappeared from history after the signing. Samuel Price Carson died in 1838 at age forty. John Turner was forced into bankruptcy and died sometime between 1844 and 1848 — even the date of his death isn't known. George Washington Barnett was killed by Indians. James Collingsworth of Tennessee, who later served as a Senator of the Republic and chief justice of its Supreme Court, might have been elected president in 1838. He ran against Mirabeau B. Lamar, but during the campaign, he killed himself by jumping into Galveston Bay.

Thomas J. Rusk was another signer who took the suicide route. He also was offered a chance to become president of the Republic, but declined. After Texas became a state, he went to Washington as one of its U. S. senators. However, he also killed himself at age fifty-two.

And what of George C. Childress, the brilliant lawyer who wrote the Declaration of Independence? He asked for a political appointment but never got it. He announced that he would write a history of the new Republic, but never got around to doing it. He set up a law practice in Houston but few clients came and he failed.

Always a man of deep melancholy and periods of high elation, he became the victim of one of his periods of mental distress. In June, 1841, he found himself in a Galveston boarding house, broke and with no funds with which to send for his new wife in Nashville or the money to go to her. He stabbed himself to death and is buried in an unmarked grave in the island city.

067310

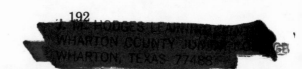

DATE DUE

GAYLORD

PRINTED IN U.S